BY SABINE BALL WITH JANICE ROGERS

Love Broke Through

Sabine's Own Story

First published by Faith Cabin Publishing 2020

First edition

ISBN: 9780692089514

Cover art by Erin Dertner/erindertner.com

This book was professionally typeset on Reedsy.
Find out more at reedsy.com

I dedicate this book to my sons, Cliff and Fred. Forgive me for my restless heart, and all the risks that I took in my life and put you through. I'm thankful that God's hands were upon you. I'm proud of the two wonderful men you have become, and your lovely wives who are raising my four grandchildren.

One generation shall praise Your works to another, And shall declare Your mighty acts.

PSALM 145:4 NKJV

Contents

Foreword

"The two most important days in a person's life is the day they are born and the day they find out WHY." —Commonly attributed to Mark Twain

*T*his is the story of Sabine Ball, who, after years of fruitless searching, finally discovered why she was born and then dedicated her life to helping others discover the same "why."

This book tells the story of an extraordinary woman, who lived through some of the most pivotal events of recent history. She grew up in Nazi Germany and participated in the girls wing of the Hitler Youth. She witnessed her city in eastern Germany being bombed and eventually coming under Soviet control. After the war, she journeyed alone to the United States as a first-generation immigrant. She married into great wealth and raised two amazing sons. She met people of great influence and impact. She was an "early adopter" of humanistic psychology and was part of the emerging hippie movement in the turbulent sixties.

But according to Sabine, her greatest achievement was the moment she made the decision to give her life to serve Jesus and to serve others on His behalf. As a result of her decision, thousands of lives have been changed, including mine.

I first met Sabine Ball while hitchhiking through a small town called Booneville, California, in the fall of 1975. I was an 18-year-old, long-haired hippie kid, seeking for God in all the wrong places. My hippie mother had moved us from San Francisco to the Mendocino Coast a few years earlier to escape the intensity of the city. We were living out the perfect back-to-the-land, New Age hippie dream. Around that time, I began hearing rumors of an infamous German woman who ran a Christian community of "Jesus freaks" on Navarro Ridge, but I never thought I would ever meet her.

Imagine how uncomfortable I was when I stuck out my thumb for a ride in Booneville and a car pulled up with Sabine sitting in the back seat. She introduced herself and told me she was just returning home after a challenging season of ministry in New York City. She asked me about my spiritual life and then proceeded to tell me about Jesus for the next 26 miles. I argued with her about religion for the entire ride, but as I stepped out of the car, she asked me if I would like to pray to receive Jesus into my life. At that moment, something shifted in my heart and I found myself saying yes. This simple prayer with Sabine Ball at the Navarro Bridge began a journey that changed my life forever. Yet I was only one of thousands of people who have been touched directly or indirectly by her life.

Somehow, Sabine caught a glimpse of God's purpose for my life and became a catalyst for my spiritual awakening. Over the next 30 years, I had the privilege of visiting with Sabine several times a year, when she was in the U.S. She became a spiritual mother, not only to me, but to my wife Diane as well. She also became a spiritual grandmother to our seven children. She helped to shape me as I grew from a young believer, to an effective leader, to a senior pastor of one of the leading churches in San Francisco. After leaving pastoral ministry, I began serving as a coach and consultant to leaders and pastors around the world, and I still credit Sabine Ball as the one who initially helped me discover the *why* of my existence.

The last time I saw Sabine was in 2007, when she spoke at our event commemorating the 40-year anniversary of the Summer of Love and the beginning of the Jesus People Movement. Her wisdom and experience were an invaluable contribution to all who attended.

*I*n the book of Hebrews, the author lists the extraordinary men and women who shaped history by serving the Lord with dedication and devotion. These saints discovered *why* they were born and gave up everything to fulfill the purpose for which they were created. The same could be said of Sabine. From her initial conversion at The Land in Mendocino to her final days of ministry in Dresden, Sabine devoted her life to Jesus. She did everything in her power to obey the Lord and lay down her life in service to others. It was told me that on the very night she passed away, she had spent the evening ministering to people on the streets of her city.

Now Sabine has joined the "great cloud of witnesses," and I am confident that her greatest desire, as we read her story, is that we would focus our attention not on Sabine Ball but rather on the One who captured her attention — Jesus. Ultimately, this is His story, portrayed in the life of an amazing woman. I pray it inspires you to walk in her footsteps as you discover her *why* and seek to make it your *why*.

Dr. Michael Brodeur
  Redding, California
  Michaelbrodeur.com

Preface

*H*ow can my entire life be captured in one book? By telling it, I hope people can identify with my story—people who have found that beauty and charm can become a trap. How quickly that happens when these qualities are used to reach self-made goals. I find this so alarming!

I'm saddened and amazed by how blind and superficial I was. But I was always searching for the truth. And through all this, I found Jesus, almost against my will. I never imagined something so wonderful.

For so many years I was against Christianity. I didn't know the One it was all about. I'm forever grateful that Tommy and the Bible opened my eyes to Him. It was God who transformed me into a new person. When my eyes were opened, I realized I had no choice but to trust in Him. My heart awoke. I suddenly had a deep reverence for the Almighty God, the Father who knows and loves me.

I follow Him because I love Him, not because He forces me. As I follow the path He lays out for me, I see unexplainable miracles, even today. I'm no longer the person who wants to stand in the spotlight, taking all the glory and attention. I want to give God all the glory. Everything that's happened since I dedicated my life to Christ, every success is due to Him. That makes my heart glad.

God knows my innermost thoughts. I want to be transparent, to let His light shine through me. He gave me the gift of new life. He's offering this to everyone. This is the message I want to share with young people. I want them to know there is a God who loves them and accepts them just as they are. He sees every person as precious.

*H*ere in Stoffwechsel, we're investing ourselves for the children and youth. Whether they know it or not, they are searching, the way I searched for so long. That's why I'm telling my story, revealing all my guilt and failures. I'm not burdened by it anymore because Jesus paid the penalty, dying on the cross. He did it because He loved me, just as He loves everyone who trusts him.

Recognizing the truth is painful, but it set me free. So, I offer this book into God's hands. I trust He will use it to change the lives of others.

Forever your friend,

Sabine

Dresden, Germany 2009

1

You are My Hiding Place

I t had been a cold day. Freezing rain was blanketing the city of Dresden as night fell on February 13,1945. Tucked safely indoors, Sabine Koritke sat darning socks, eager to finish and go to bed. The terrors of the war were far away. In the next room, she could hear the gentle snores of her nine-year-old brother, Hans, worn out after a day of great excitement. It was *carnivale* and Sabine and Hans had joyfully run through the old alleyways and streets of Dresden, their laughter bouncing off cupolas and turrets of eighteenth-century buildings.

The two siblings had enjoyed themselves even though the crowds had been smaller and more subdued this year. The Soviet Army was only sixty miles away, but everyone hoped for the best. Exquisite Dresden had changed in only a few weeks' time, its population doubling to well over a million as refugees poured in from the east. Dresden was not only a hospital center. It also held 26,000 Allied prisoners of war. These facts, added to the lack of military targets and the city's status as a cultural treasure, made everyone believe they were

1

safe in Dresden.

And no one felt more safe, more hopeful than the young. Like nineteen-year-old Sabine and her little brother Hans.

Sabine moved the needle rhythmically back and forth through the black sock as she thought about Christmas back home in East Prussia. It wasn't quite eight weeks ago.

They had decided to lay aside their sadness over the eldest child, Marianne, and have a real Christmas one more time.

Their Konigsberg house glowed with candles Mother had placed throughout the living room. Flickering flames danced everywhere—on the antique mahogany table with its elaborately carved legs, on the small desk, and on the dark, highly polished surfaces of their grand piano.

Oh, how Sabine hated that piano, just as she dreaded the suffocating lessons with prim Fräulein Richau. How she resented the endless hours, struggling to make her fingers follow the notes in her orange *etude* book. But on Christmas she liked the piano, covered as it was with Mother's candles.

Sabine reached for the next pair of Hans' socks and smiled to herself. He had received them for Christmas and already they were riddled with holes. When these socks were new, no one could have guessed how soon war would overwhelm their family.

Well, Sabine mused, *perhaps Father expected it.* He must have been planning his family's escape from the advancing Red Army. Sabine put fresh thread in the darning needle. She could still hear her father's strong voice on Christmas Eve, reading the story of Jesus' birth. He didn't believe what he read from the Bible. But it was tradition. After he finished the last verse, they joined in the hymn they always sang: "Glory to God in the highest and peace on Earth...."

Immediately after New Year's, Father put her and Hans on an overcrowded refugee train and sent them to the presumed safety of Dresden and the Schlüter family.

Her parents trusted the Schlüters. They owned a large bread mill, and their products were known throughout Germany. Schlüter bread nourished the Reich. The Schlüter house on Franz Liszt Strasse would be a safe haven until Father and Mother could send for them.

A piercing wail shattered the silence, pulling Sabine from her reverie. She groaned. It was 9:30 pm and an air raid warning was disturbing another night.

"Hans!" she cried, leaping into action. Air raids were almost routine now. Sabine reached for the brown leather suitcase she kept packed for such occasions. Inside was their most important possession–Mother's jewelry. It was a small asset, but their only nest egg. They would need it to help them survive whatever the future held.

"Hans!" she called again, sharper this time. "Get up! Into the cellar!"

With one hand she clutched the suitcase tightly, and with the other she firmly grasped the still sleepy Hans, rushing for the stairs. "It'll be okay," she whispered.

She felt little panic–just an urgency to get to safety. Dresden would not be destroyed. Not the *Elbeflorenz*—"Florence along the Elbe River"—famous for delicate china, art and music, and a horizon crowded with steeples and spires, centered by the massive dome of Frauenkirche. Surely the British and Americans would spare this cultural treasure. Their planes would fly on to Berlin as usual.

As Sabine and Hans ran down the staircase, the first bombs pummeled the city. The house took a violent jolt. Sabine gripped Hans tighter, flying down the stairs, stumbling more steps than they actually took. A terrible roar made her want to envelop him, but there was no time.

Quickly they fell into the cellar, slamming the trapdoor behind them. She glanced around the small room, slowly counting all the silent figures hovering in the flickering candlelight. Sabine pulled Hans close, feeling his soft cheek next to hers. It calmed her a little and she squeezed his hand tightly.

The entire Schlüter family had made it to the drafty cellar—all but Father Schlüter. He was at the mill. Was that also a target?

Once more the earth shuddered as another bomb exploded nearby. Inside the safety of the cellar, it was impossible to know how close the bombs were falling. Each detonation felt like an earthquake. However, the Schlüters had a good bomb shelter. Steel reinforced the ceiling and walls.

Hans poked her. "Sabine," he whispered, "Are you afraid?"

She squeezed his hand tighter, nodding her assent. Sheer terror was coursing through her. Not so much the fear of death, but the *process* of death. Would they be buried alive or burn in flames?

As the endless night wore on, anger began to crowd out her fear. Had she and Hans fled to Dresden, leaving behind those they loved most, only to die in this miserable cellar?

She remembered the hardships they endured to reach Dresden. When they arrived at the overflowing train, the aisles were so filled they couldn't enter through the doors.

Before addressing that problem, Father asked Sabine, "Do you have the list in a safe place, Sabine?"

She nodded, pointing inside her shirt. He had given her a

list of friends and addresses in various cities. If the invaders came too close in one place, she and Hans could flee to another. Eventually, their parents would follow and find them. It was typical of Father to think of every contingency.

Father hugged his two children. Then, his whole body trembling from exertion, he lifted her high, then Hans, shoving them into the train through a window.

For hours Sabine and Hans rode through the wintry countryside, jammed in like cattle. The smell of so many people pressed together soon became an unbearable stench. When Sabine realized she urgently needed to use the toilet, she waited for hours as the train lumbered along. Finally, her pain became unbearable. She pushed her way through to the toilet, only to discover the tiny room was occupied by four passengers! With her face burning, she had no choice but to relieve herself in front of them.

*****

Another jolt brought her mind back to Dresden and their present misery. The cellar's earthen walls shook as bombs continued to pound the city. Beams and supports groaned. Sabine could hear people screaming in the streets above them. Then, all was quiet. The volley of bombs was over. From far away the "all clear" signal sounded faintly.

The little group waited another five minutes before creeping up the stairs. They breathed a sigh of relief when they saw the Schlüter house was still standing. But the windows had all been blown out and the doors were torn from their hinges.

Somehow Sabine knew they had to get out of Dresden–immediately, even though it was the dark of night, in the middle of winter. With Hans still clinging tightly to her hand, she told Frau Schlüter, "We're leaving."

The older woman's eyes filled with tears. "No, darling. It's late. Tomorrow we'll all be thinking more clearly."

Sabine reluctantly agreed to wait until morning.

"Besides," Frau Schlüter added, "Dresden is in ruins. The enemy need not come anymore."

However, they did come again–only three hours later, and with a fury no one expected. Sabine and Hans ran into the Schlüter bomb shelter again. She looked around in the darkness. This time strangers had also crowded into the cellar. Many were wounded and burned.

The bombs became one continuous explosion, slamming into the city above them. Sabine felt something inside her go on autopilot. She helped to bandage the injured while listening to whispered prayers all around. But they went no farther than the cellar ceiling.

What utter nonsense, she thought. If she wasn't an atheist by this point, she would become one. *Where is God on a night like this?*

Again and again the planes came, and hot air penetrated the cellar. Then someone screamed, "The house is on fire!" Panic flooded the shelter.

As one, they ran up the steps, stopping suddenly at the top. A scorching blast slammed into Sabine's face. As they ran into the street, she choked, trying to breathe.

Someone found wet cloths, and Sabine wrapped them around her head and Hans'.

Then Sabine shouted, "The suitcase!" In their haste, she had forgotten it inside the cellar. She left Hans standing at the side of the street and plunged back into the burning building.

Seconds later, she emerged with it under her arm. Hans cried when he saw her, great tears rolling down his blackened cheeks.

They plunged into the street. Which way should they run? Everywhere was an inferno. The sky was blood red. It felt like the air itself was on fire. Every tree and every bush burned. Hot winds sucked through the city, like a fire tornado, ripping off roofs and tossing cars and trucks about like toys.

Sheer horror took over the city. The most awful sight was people running and screaming while flames consumed them. Survivors scrambled about, desperately searching for lost loved ones. Children sobbed for their mothers and mothers wailed for lost children.

Sabine and Hans found an old bicycle leaning forlornly against a lamppost, its owner no longer able to come for it. They placed their suitcase on the bike and began to pick their way out of the city.

As they passed burning shells of buildings, they tried not to breathe the acrid smoke. The smell of phosphorous and burning flesh was everywhere. When they reached a small hill, not far from what had been the Schlüter's house, they collapsed in exhaustion. Here they were somewhat safe from walls of fire and whipping currents that set asphalt roads ablaze, and flowed up and down stairs.

Sabine looked around. People who had survived with only their lives surrounded them on the hill. It was a nightmare of hell. Would she ever wake?

Later, they learned Herr Schlüter had perished in his mill. He was one of a multitude of casualties. Many people literally melted inside of bomb shelters. Reports put the number of Dresden dead somewhere between twenty-five and forty thousand. But others said more than one hundred thousand died. It was impossible to know.

Sabine would never forget that night. As she and Hans gazed over the sea of fire, she made up her mind. She must not only get out of Dresden. She had to escape Germany.

2

Everything is Meaningless

The cold of night deepened as Sabine and Hans trudged down the road. They were two small figures joining a pitiful stream of survivors leaving Dresden. As she walked, images of Adolf Hitler invaded Sabine's mind again and again. All during her teenage years, he had been so great and imposing, even indestructible. His pictures were everywhere. He was the one who would usher in a thousand years of peace for the Fatherland.

Every week during her teens she attended the *Bund Deutscher Mädel*—the female branch of Hitler Youth. The more she attended, the more the idea of Hitler took hold of her. Many of her friends imagined themselves head over heels in love with him. But Sabine's feelings were different. There was something about his unshakable authority—menacing, yet strangely attractive.

Sabine had a weakness for strong men. This was why she felt a shiver of excitement whenever she thought of Hitler. His virtues were extolled by all–on the radio, during youth lectures called *Jugendstunden,* even by her teachers at school. Sabine felt intimately connected to him. It was Hitler the mythic hero, Hitler who led Germany out of the ashes of defeat after the Great War. Sabine had felt the call. She knew she should follow, obey, and serve without question.

Now, as she and Hans fled the charred ruins of Dresden, her image of Hitler shattered into a million pieces. It was like losing part of herself. Hitler was no longer all powerful. Now she knew it was an illusion. She felt so betrayed. And what about her belief that the Nazis were changing the face of history? Was it all one monstrous lie?

She remembered an evening six years ago, back home in Königsberg. It was eight o'clock, and she and Marianne, her older sister by two years, were already in bed. They were just drifting off to sleep when Father surprised them by calling, "Come into the living room, my daughters!"

Puzzled, the two girls ran to the sitting room. They stood before Father in their warm nightgowns. He looked sad.

"Listen to this, Daughters." He turned up the radio. It was someone on the BBC, speaking in crisp tones: "German forces have invaded Czechoslovakia...."

In her mind, Sabine automatically substituted the word "freed," just as she had been taught in school. German forces had *freed* Czechoslovakia.

They listened with Father as the BBC reporter condemned Germany's actions. Sabine could hardly believe her ears! How could a foreign radio program spread such lies? Clearly the English didn't grasp Germany's wonderful mission.

Father turned off the radio and faced his daughters. His next words floored Sabine. "I don't believe the English news. But I don't believe the German news, either. Hitler is a fraud."

What? Hitler a fraud? It was as if Father had declared the world was flat. How could he say such a terrible thing? She had always adored her father. He was smart, educated and well-read. Up until that moment, his wisdom was unquestionable. But now there was no escaping the fact. *Father is a traitor!*

Then he told the girls, "Never speak of these matters. It's important that you know the truth. But it's just as important that you never tell anyone what I just said. One can never be too careful."

Back in their bedroom, the sisters held each other, weeping. Sabine had never sobbed so hard. She felt a ripping deep in her soul as she was torn between her father and her beloved Hitler.

*****

Now as they left the city, a bitter taste came to her mouth. Her father had been right. Sabine saw it all with terrible clarity. Her idol had clay feet. As she pushed the bicycle along the road, a sickness reached the pit of her stomach. *I entrusted my heart to a fraud.* She had been lied to, used and abused. What would become of her and little Hans now?

She looked and saw her brother was crying. Big tears streaked down his sooty face. "I want to go home," he whimpered over and over. "I want to go home."

Sabine reached her arms around his shaking shoulders.

Suddenly Hans looked up as if struck by a new terror. "Where are Mommy and Daddy?"

This tore into her heart as she was forced to face questions she had been pushing aside. Their parents—what had happened to them? And what about their dear servant, Ella? Were they safe in Königsberg? Had a similar attack happened there?

She could only stroke Hans' blond hair, darkened with Dresden's ashes. "I don't know, Hans." She wiped the tears from his cheeks. "I don't know."

Gripping Hans' hand firmly, Sabine used her other hand to slowly push the bicycle. She was glad Father's list of friends was safely inside her shirt. She wasn't sure where they would head next. In any case, it was away from Dresden.

They slogged through the night until a bitterly cold dawn. As they came upon an old farmhouse, the farmer's wife, a bedraggled crone with a gentle smile, met them at the door. She gave Hans a cup of warm milk and Sabine threw her a pleading look. What they desperately needed now was rest. The farmer's wife understood and nodded. They could stay in the barn, at least for a couple of days.

As Sabine drifted off to sleep on the sweet-smelling hay, the question continued to haunt her. *What had happened to their parents?* For weeks before the bombing, they had heard nothing. As the Soviet Army swept through eastern Germany, telephone lines were down and mail was uncertain. Surely Father and Mother escaped East Prussia.

She clung to that hope and sank into a dreamless sleep.

As she and Hans spent the coming days at the farmhouse recuperating, the question of their parents' fate nagged at Sabine. She reminded herself of their last telephone call. Mother, Father, and Ella were going to leave on the luxury ocean liner, the *Wilhelm Gustloff*.

The *Wilhelm Gustloff* had been the dream ship of the thirties, playing a central role in Nazi propaganda. A floating colossus, 208 meters long and 56 meters high, with ten decks and lacquered in princely white, it sported a swimming pool and a dance floor. Built for two thousand passengers, it was a key feature of the government program, *Kraft durch Freude*—power through pleasure, or KdF.

The central aim of the KdF was to provide everyone with affordable leisure activities, such as concerts and theater, day trips, libraries, and vacations. They even planned a state-of-the-art amusement park in Rügen. Tens of millions of Germans took advantage of KdF, workers just as much as academics. The government promised the "result for all would be power, strength, and efficiency." Of course, it also strengthened the regime's hold. While the citizens were holidaying, they were also under government control.

However, as the war dragged on, KdF programs, including the *Wilhelm Gustloff,* suffered deprivations. The once white giant, so central to Nazi pride, was now painted gray. In early 1945, the ship transported refugees fleeing from the advancing Red Army.

As the Russians pushed farther and farther into Germany, they took their revenge, setting fires, pillaging, and raping. It was a terrifying time for the German people. Sabine's father, Herr Koritke, owned the largest transshipping company in East Prussia. But by now, all his warehouses were lost. The war—the "German madness" as he thought of it—had destroyed his life's work. Like many others, he began to make plans to escape his homeland.

The first part of Father's plan had been set in motion when he sent his beloved children, Sabine and Hans, on the jam-packed train headed westward. That was the last time Sabine had seen her parents. Contact had been very difficult since the end of January.

Her parents planned to find another way out of Königsberg as soon as possible. Sabine knew this would be gut-wrenching for them. It meant leaving their eldest child behind, forever. Marianne had died from tuberculosis a year ago. She caught

13

the disease while serving as a nurse with the Red Cross. Sabine knew her parents would never completely recover from Marianne's death. Especially her mother. She had always been distant to Sabine, but very close to Marianne. And if they left Königsberg, a large part of her heart would remain buried in the churchyard with her eldest daughter.

Escape by land had become increasingly difficult. Then salvation came in the *Gustloff*, which lay in Danzig Bay. German citizens could sail the Baltic Sea to safer Reich territory, possibly Kiel or Flensburg. It was better to travel by ship than by foot through snow and ice, facing possible frostbite. As far as Sabine knew, her parents had obtained tickets for the *Wilhelm Gustloff*.

*****

History would later show that at first, everyone boarding the *Wilhelm Gustloff* proceeded in an orderly fashion. But before departure, a great multitude began to swarm the dock. The atmosphere deteriorated. People forced their way onto the ship, shoving ticket holders aside. It was chaos. There was no way the ship could hold all the desperate refugees—mostly women, children, and the elderly.

It was every person for himself. The lucky ones pushed their way onboard, leaving thousands of frantic people behind.

The *Wilhelm Gustloff* put to sea at noon on January 30, 1945. But with about ten thousand souls aboard, she was hopelessly overfilled, far exceeding her capacity of two thousand.

On the promenade deck, originally created for strolling, passengers packed in next to one another. As the ship sailed from the harbor, many wiped away tears as they took one final look back at Prussia. Who knew how long it would be until they could return?

3

We Wait in Hope for the Lord

Sabine waited at the farmhouse, clinging to hope. Surely they would be reunited with their parents soon. Still, as the days passed, anxiety nibbled at her soul.

She and Hans said goodbye to the farm woman. Sabine checked Father's list again, choosing an address in Dessau. They managed to board a freight train headed in that direction. It was frigid in the drafty car as they rumbled over the rails, but they finally reached the city. At least they knew a place where they'd be welcomed.

Sabine and Hans made their way to a gracious villa, home of her old school friend, Inge Kleppel. Sabine and Inge had become fast friends while attending boarding school.

Inge flung the door open and gave them a big hug. "It was right to come here," she said.

All the girls from Reinhardswaldschule, the top boarding school in Kassel, came from good homes, including Inge Kleppel. Her father was director of Junkers Werke, a company that built aircraft and motors. Director Kleppel made sure the company ran like a well-oiled machine. Since Junkers Werke was an important cog in the wheel of the Reich, keeping the war moving, Inge's father was well-connected to Hermann Göring, second in Nazi command and designated successor to Adolf Hitler. Thus, Sabine had landed in high society.

Despite the sanctuary of the Kleppel mansion, Sabine couldn't shake her unease. *Where are Father and Mother? And Ella?*

She shared her fears with Frau Kleppel one morning at breakfast, before Hans had gotten up. Sabine said she was worried. "They should be here by now. They had booked passage on the *Gustloff*."

Frau Kleppel's face went white.

"The *Gustloff*? Darling Sabine," She reached across the table and took her hand. "I heard someone say the *Gustloff* sank. Three weeks ago."

Sabine went numb. It couldn't be true. Frau Kleppel must have heard it wrong! Desperately, she ran through the town, questioning anyone she could. The more people she asked, the more a terrible reality took shape. At last, she found the newspaper office. They let her read a copy of the paper with the story of the ill-fated ship. She took a seat at an empty desk and unfolded the paper. The words swam before her eyes as she read how the *Gustloff* sailed from its harbor on January 30th. That evening, a Soviet U-boat hit the *Gustloff* with three torpedoes. The ship reeled and within sixty minutes, disappeared into the inky, freezing water.

Oh God! No!

She read on. It was the greatest shipping disaster in history. More than nine thousand perished, six times as many as on the *Titanic*. Half were children.

Sabine lowered the paper, her hands shaking violently. *What about survivors?*

She read further. A quickly dispatched boat, the *T36* was able to scoop up little more than a thousand. Sabine held her breath, quickly running her finger down the list of those rescued. Just to make sure, she read through the list again.

No one with the last name of "Koritke" was there.

Sabine fought her rising panic. She wasn't the only one who had no idea if her loved ones were dead or alive. Because of the chaotic boarding of the *Gustloff*, no one compiled a passenger list. It was impossible to tell who had found their grave in the frigid waters of the Baltic that night.

The ship sank on the twelfth anniversary of the Nazis coming to power. Hitler's radio speech had been broadcast onboard the *Gustloff*. He exhorted the German people "to make the heart stronger than ever before," no matter the circumstances.

The *Führer's* words became a sheer mockery in the ears of those who met their death moments later.

In the newspaper office, Sabine recoiled in disbelief and shock. Had her family perished? What was her future? Where would they go? What would they do? And how could she tell Hans?

She decided for the time being to say nothing. Since there was no official word of their parents' death, there was still a shred of hope.

In the coming days, she clung to that. When Hans whimpered, asking about their parents, she continued to answer with one word. "Soon." Every evening she sat at his bed, gently rubbing his back before tucking him in. They both knew she was no substitute for Mother. Often Hans sobbed, homesick and longing for their parents.

Sabine could have cried along with him. Why couldn't things be as they were before? She wanted to be back home in Königsberg, among the roses cared for by their gardener. His name was Erwin and he had fallen in love with Grete, her first nanny. After Grete and Erwin married and left, Ella had come into their home—beloved Ella.

The Koritkes had such a wonderful home–a life without worries, so happy, so uncomplicated. Besides having a gardener and nannies, many others lovingly cared for their needs. There was the washerwoman and the dressmaker who came regularly, and a kindly doctor who made house calls.

Doctor Klein was Jewish. Her family was indebted to him, because years before he had saved Hans' life. They ignored the decree barring Jewish physicians from practicing medicine.

Sabine would never forget the day Mother appeared at the family table, her face etched with grief. When they asked her what was the matter, Mother fled the room in tears. When she came back, drying her tears, she told of seeing Dr. Klein on the tram. His jacket bore a yellow star. Mother said she had held his hands, trying to comfort him.

As the government increased their persecution of the Jews, Mother sent parcels of provisions to her Jewish friends in Berlin—always without a return address. She repeatedly sent gifts to Dr. Klein, too.

However, they never heard from Dr. Klein again.

*****

Now, a few short years later in the Kleppel villa, Sabine found herself once again sitting beside Hans' bed, their nightly tuck-in ritual completed. So much had turned their world upside down. She didn't dare think of the future. Ever since escaping Dresden, she had forgotten how to dream.

18

Hans had just fallen asleep when she heard a sound in the doorway. Looking up, she saw Inge with a mischievous smile dancing across her face.

"Shhh!" Sabine put her finger to her lips, then pointed at Hans.

Inge grinned, motioning for Sabine to follow her. Tiptoeing so as not to wake Hans, Sabine slipped away after her, hurrying down the stairs. Halfway down, she stopped and stared at a figure at the bottom.

"Father!"

She sprang down the last steps and fell into her father's arms. Mother and Ella stood next to him, with a few meager belongings on the floor.

Mother hurried upstairs to wake Hans up. After welcoming them, the Kleppels withdrew, giving them some privacy. Sabine's family gathered around the dining table. Hans sat on Mother's lap with happy tears flowing down his cheeks. Over cups of hot tea, they pieced together their story.

They had left Königsberg on an earlier boat, two days before the doomed *Wilhelm Gustloff*. Upon their safe arrival, they had stayed fourteen days in Rauschen.

"The Russians were getting very close," Father said, his voice shaking with emotion.

When Sabine mentioned their original plans, to sail on the *Gustloff*, Father said, "A fortunate turn of events!"

Sabine knew he was no believer. He didn't accuse God nor reproach him because of the war. But he didn't thank him for saving them from death in the Baltic Sea, either. He just said, "We were lucky."

He told how they made it to Berlin. There they learned of the fire bombing of Dresden. Mother's eyes were haunted.

"We tried to contact the Schlüters, but it was impossible to find where our children were."

She reached over and squeezed Sabine's hand.

Father said they had guessed Sabine and Hans might be in Dessau. Listening to her family's tale as they huddled around the table, Sabine felt a warm glow of gratitude well up. She looked over at Hans who had fallen asleep in his mother's arms. Who knew how long this moment of peace would last?

4

I Reduced You to Ashes

As the Allies kept up their air attacks, the Kleppels and Koritkes fell into a pattern. Every time the siren's wail pierced the air, they sprang into action. Following an all-too-familiar routine, they fled outside and around to the cellar door, then back under the mansion, into the basement. Once safely there, they waited on hard wooden benches.

*****

It was the evening of the day the Americans crossed the Rhine at Remagen, March 7, 1945. Planes came thundering over Dessau and the families ran down to the cellar.

Herr Kleppel arrived with his chauffeur, joining them in the basement. He brought a small, battery-powered radio with him—a personal gift from Göring himself. As the radio crackled, they crowded around it, desperate for information. What was happening in the world above them?

And yet, they all felt so beaten down. It no longer mattered if the Allies were advancing. All that mattered was survival, nothing else. They sank onto the benches in the cellar.

Over the radio, they heard the throaty voice of Zarah

Leander singing, "I know one day a miracle will happen."

They had long since lost their faith in miracles.

Sabine glanced at her family, sitting on one side. Even in these circumstances, it was good to be together again. Hans was pressed against Mother, her arms laced tightly around him. Father sat stone-faced, his hands inside his coat pockets.

Watching her father, Sabine felt reassured. She knew that inside his coat pocket, his hand was wrapped tightly around a revolver. Sabine was absolutely certain. If worse came to worst, her father wouldn't allow her to suffer. He would shoot her first.

Sabine no longer feared death. What she did fear was suffering. Being burned alive. She didn't want to beg for death, as she had seen people do in Dresden. And so, every time a bomb hit above them, Sabine looked quickly at her father.

He sat resolutely, his hand never leaving his pocket. He was the guardian of his family.

Suddenly a deafening roar exploded through the cellar. The Kleppel's house had taken a direct hit! They could hear the horrifying sound of beams snapping overhead. Sabine knew they had mere minutes to get out or be buried alive.

As they raced up the stairs, Sabine was overtaken by a terrifying numbness. Her emotions were shoved aside and the survival routine took over completely.

They assembled in the garden, staring as flames engulfed the house. Again and again, bomber squadrons tore through the night sky, leaving streaks of light against velvet blackness. Then they were gone, and only the blazing house illumined the darkness.

They watched helplessly as the great house burned, the

flickering light dancing over their faces. Sabine couldn't turn away from the awesome sight. They looked through a huge picture window as the fire moved insatiably through the great house, consuming doors, stairs, and furniture without prejudice. It engulfed drapes and emptied wine glasses on the table.

Then the flames lapped around the grand piano. As if performing one final symphony, sheets of music floated into the air, dancing through the room before crumpling to their fiery death. The wallpaper curled, dissolving from the walls. Then, the piano began to burn red and gold.

Inge and Sabine stood silently next to one another, arm in arm. For a moment, Sabine felt as if they were being treated to a final concert of Chopin or Mozart. She could almost imagine the clouds of smoke taking on the image of a pianist wearing a tailcoat, sitting down and placing his fingers one last time upon the keys.

"Look," Inge pointed at a photograph of herself smiling, still sitting on the piano. Sabine was mesmerized as Inge's picture refused to burn. Even as the room was in flames all around, the photo of smiling Inge remained. It was grotesque.

Sabine felt like crying. How many times had they stood in this very garden? Watching the fire was almost like watching an attraction at one of the Kleppel's many garden parties. Only, this night it was a scene from hell and no one had a champagne glass in hand.

Herr Kleppel had been drinking–Sabine could smell the alcohol on his breath. As he gazed at the flames he began to laugh, quietly at first, then with increasing intensity. It was an unnatural, hysterical laugh that turned Sabine's spine to water.

So far, Director Kleppel had grown rich from the war. Now Germany's defeat was even reaching him. He wasn't just witnessing the engulfing of his home. It was the unraveling of his life. A few weeks later, Americans brought him to a detention center. He never left again.

*****

Within an hour, nothing remained of the magnificent villa other than charred walls and ash. Even Inge's photo had surrendered to the fire. Once again, Sabine and her family found themselves homeless.

As she stood there shivering beside the ruined mansion, Sabine make a silent promise to herself. Somehow she would flee Germany.

The following weeks sped by. Two things were clear, though. The war was nearly over and Germany was crushed. Sabine also felt defeated. Her experiences in Dresden and in Dessau left her traumatized and vulnerable.

After Germany surrendered, Sabine's family moved to Ichenhausen, near Günzburg in the western part of Bavaria. They were fortunate to end up in an American-occupied zone. Some of their friends in Konigsberg were now trapped behind Soviet lines, in East Germany.

A married couple who were both doctors kindly offered them shelter. The entire Koritke family and Ella crowded into one spare bedroom.

Still, their situation was better than the wretched souls in a nearby camp for displaced persons. Some of the refugees were Jews. Stories began to emerge, mainly from doctors who worked among them. They were terrible stories–of gas chambers and ovens, and piles of Jewish bodies.

The Koritke family was horrified, unwilling to believe it. But

24

finally, there was no escaping the truth of what had happened. Sabine felt embarrassed and ashamed to be German.

Her family was struggling each day to survive and rise above the war's terrible aftermath. Sabine thought of how much they had endured since Christmas–so much disruption and hardship. And no one more so than Father. His home and his life's work—his large shipping agency—had been destroyed. If anyone had a reason to be bitter, it was he. However, he seemed content, even here in their humbling circumstances. Surely she could get through it, too.

Sabine began to look for a job.

One day she passed by some American soldiers, an island of clean, pressed uniforms in a sea of burned out rubble. Sabine offered a brief smile and hurried past. But one soldier called out to her.

"Are you interested in a job, miss?" he asked politely in accented German.

She glanced at him and decided he was serious.

"Yes, I am," she replied, mustering her courage to speak to an American soldier for the first time. There was no need to tell him she had spent the entire day looking for work, to no avail.

The job turned out to be furnishing an American officers' club. The actual work made her uncomfortable, but she was in no position to refuse employment. They were told to take furniture from the homes of those formerly in Nazi power. A soldier of the occupation said to select the finest pieces of furniture.

After only one day, Sabine was in tears. She couldn't walk into people's homes and take their furniture! They may have been Nazis, but they were still her countrymen–people just

25

like the Kleppels, who had sheltered them.

Eventually, the Americans arranged for another German girl to do the actual selection. Sabine's job was to arrange this "new" furniture in the officers' club.

Sabine was surprised to discover she had a knack for decorating. In another time, unblemished by burned out buildings and deprivation, perhaps she would have studied interior design. However, with the present chaos in Germany, she couldn't take classes.

Thankfully, Father was also able to find work. After months of searching, he found a position with a large shipping company. It wasn't as good as being the owner of a shipping company. But in their reduced circumstances, it was a welcome relief.

Slowly but surely, the Koritkes were emerging from the ashes. Sabine also began to rebuild her life. As the years passed, she became more accustomed to this new life. Yet she held onto her promise to leave Germany. She was counting the days until she could start a new life. Germany, as she had once known and loved it, was gone.

One evening on her way home, Sabine caught her reflection in a newly repaired shop window. A tall, attractive girl with dark hair and brown eyes stared back at her. Sabine smoothed her nearly threadbare coat. *I want more than this*, she thought. *I want to enjoy life. I want to wear lovely clothes and meet charming people. I'm too young to work this hard just to survive.*

Then with breathtaking speed, her wish was granted in 1949.

5

The Lord is Good

Sabine took in the salty smell of the sea and felt the cool wind in her hair. She was happy, but tears spilled down her cheeks. She grasped the back rail of the *General Blatchford*. The ship was taking her to a new life. She stared hard at the North Sea Coast, trying to memorize every detail. Homes along the shore became small, then tiny. The beach turned into a sandy smudge on the easel of the horizon.

The boat rolled as it broke through an exceptionally large wave, causing sea water to crash onto the deck, across her feet. She shivered in clothes that were much too thin, even though it was August. She should go and find her cabin, but she couldn't tear herself away from the rail and that last glimpse of home. Then the shoreline disappeared into the sea. It was a fitting goodbye to her old life.

Sabine was nearly twenty-four. Four years had passed since the end of the war. Four long years in which she had planned, dreamed, and hoped to get away. Her parents didn't try to stop her. They knew she wanted something more. And now, as the *Blatchford* crested a wave, she thought, *There's no going back.*

What's waiting on the other side of the ocean? Where will I go and what will I do?

Sabine didn't consider what a striking picture she made, standing at the railing, clutching her battered brown suitcase. She always ignored admiring glances from others. She wouldn't admit she was pretty, even though her face was chiseled with high cheekbones and her fair skin was delicate. Dimples danced beside her mouth when she smiled. The fact that she was so unaware of her beauty made her all the more appealing.

Her stomach began to lurch. She ran inside to a toilet, barely making it before the first heave.

A long while later, she continued to cling to the toilet, her forehead soaked with perspiration. *I don't know if I want to get well or just die!*

Eventually, she felt stable enough to make her way on shaky legs to her cabin. Her spirits fell as she took in what would be her home for the next several weeks.

Certainly, the word "cabin" was an overstatement. No one would call the ship's accommodations luxurious. The *Blatchford* was an old warship that cruised under the American flag. Sabine's cabin consisted of a dingy gray cot, crammed dormitory-style among the beds of forty other women. There would be no solitude on this voyage!

Already, the sour smell of vomit wafted throughout the room, making Sabine's stomach wrench again.

At least I don't have to sleep on the floor, she thought with a wry grin, trying to put a positive spin on things.

Her surroundings were less than ideal, but at least they were temporary. She was on her way to America, on her way to a new life!

Climbing onto her cot, Sabine pulled the itchy wool blanket over her head to block out the fetid smell. Immediately, she fell into a dreamless sleep.

She woke several hours later, feeling surprisingly refreshed. Miraculously, her stomach no longer heaved. Even the dormitory didn't smell quite as bad. She headed for the upper deck.

The cool fresh air brought welcome relief. Bright sunlight ran over the dancing waves and Sabine felt once more that the world held promise.

Several others also stood on the deck, staring out to sea. Sabine noticed many had aquiline noses and dark curly hair. Like most of the passengers, they were Jewish—the handful who had escaped with their lives. Sabine tried to imagine the hardships they had endured. Deep lines cut into their faces, and they stooped as if they were still carrying heavy burdens.

She shuddered and turned away. The entire world—including Sabine—was now aware of the atrocities Hitler's regime had committed. How horrified she had been to learn of the concentration camps, of the ovens, and the tall chimneys. How could anyone in her country, her beloved Germany, have committed these sins against innocent people?

Hitler's legacy was a huge stain on her homeland. As she passed the Jews onboard, Sabine was ashamed. She decided that from then on, when anyone asked her nationality, she would say "Austrian." How else could she start her new life?

A more terrifying thought struck Sabine. Many of her countrymen had committed atrocities. Surely, their hands were stained with innocent blood. *But what about my hands?* she thought. *Do I bear any responsibility for crimes committed by others?*

She remembered their comfortable life before, and yet how helpless they had been to protect people like their kindly physician, Dr. Klein. Then she recalled Hitler's stirring speeches on the radio, and the thrilling strains of the Nazi hymn, the "Horst Wessel." *Do I share even the smallest amount of blame for what happened?*

Even though she tried to deny it, Sabine knew in her heart of hearts, at least on an emotional level, she was guilty. She had let Hitler capture her soul. She bore guilt.

On that long ocean voyage, Sabine also recognized she had been a victim of Hitler, too. The incessant propaganda and the hypnotic pull of the crowd had brainwashed her, carrying her and the rest of the German youth on a wave of hysteria, confusion, and wickedness, leaving them washed up on the shore.

The war was over, her country lay in rubble, and her identity was shattered. Now, she wondered. *Who is Sabine Koritke?*

Day after day, Sabine held onto the railing and stared at the horizon, trying to grasp a mystery just beyond her reach. She hadn't found it during the years after the war, and she couldn't find it now. Perhaps once she began her new life as an American, maybe then she would have the answer.

Sabine knew her fellow passengers had more terrible scars. She could see it in their eyes. They had seen the worst that human beings could do to one another. They had known true evil.

She wanted to reach out to them, to try and comfort them. But her German identity hung heavily on her shoulders. All she could do was secretly watch as the Jews sat in silence. What memories taunted them, Sabine couldn't even fathom. Camps with barbed wire, guards in black boots? Perhaps they had survived by helping herd their own people into gas chambers. Maybe they sat in silent mourning for lost loved ones, those who had perished without even a gravestone to mark their passing.

Sabine often took refuge at the stern of the ship. There she stood, lost in thought. As far as she could see, in every direction, there was only water. Yet with every minute, the distance between her and Germany became greater.

*****

As they neared their destination, Sabine found herself standing at the rail again, this time surrounded by many other passengers. A shout of excitement surged through the group, as far off in distance, land slowly came into view. It was Boston.

America!

She found herself caught up in the joy of the moment. All around her, people were laughing, their arms gesturing as they spoke in half a dozen languages. A young mother next to her cried silent tears, holding her tiny child close.

As she disembarked, a wall of intense August heat and humidity hit her. She didn't know what she had expected, but the greeting she received was anything but cordial. An efficient group of women dressed in the blue and white uniforms of the Red Cross greeted the passengers without a smile, ordering them into lines. One woman was angry that most of newcomers couldn't speak English.

Sabine was grateful for the English she had learned in her exclusive boarding school. It took several hours to make her way through all the bureaucratic red tape. She inched from line to line. Long waits were punctuated by Sabine hurriedly showing her documents. Rubber stamps slammed down on papers.

Then she was pushed into another line to start the process all over again. She was exhausted by the time she reached the final line, dragging all her worldly possessions in her old brown suitcase. But all that mattered was, she had arrived. She was in America.

6

You are My Refuge

Sabine headed for New York City and the home of Aunt Mary. As she sat on the cramped train, the heat was stifling. The humidity soaked through her clothes. Just being on a train made her stomach cramp, bringing back memories of terrible train trips in war torn Germany.

Reaching into her satchel, she retrieved a worn photograph, fingering it nervously. A fashionably dressed woman smiled back from the picture. Had Aunt Mary changed much since she had seen her last? Mary Lobel wasn't really her aunt, but a dear, old friend of Mother. Many times during Sabine's childhood, right up until the start of the war, Aunt Mary had crossed the Atlantic to visit the Koritkes. During the war, she faithfully sent parcels to help out the family. Sabine wondered if she knew how much her gifts had meant to them.

"Utterly delighted!" Aunt Mary had replied when Sabine wrote and told her she was coming to the United States. What's more, she had agreed to be Sabine's guarantor with U.S. Immigration.

Butterflies fluttered through Sabine's stomach as her train

pulled into New York City. From the window, she could see Aunt Mary on the platform. She stood tall and proud, a yellow pillbox hat placed smartly on her head. Sabine would have known her anywhere.

As Sabine stepped off the train, Aunt Mary rushed to meet her. A broad smile creased her face as Sabine curtsied low, remembering her Prussian manners even in the midst of Grand Central Station.

"Welcome, child!" Aunt Mary swept her into a big hug. How wonderful physical contact felt. It was the first time anyone had touched her in weeks. They stepped out together into the blaze of New York sunshine.

Sabine was immediately overwhelmed by the city, by the hustle and bustle, by the vibrant energy that flowed all around her. Aunt Mary expertly hailed a cab and soon they arrived at her home in Brooklyn. Sabine looked around the apartment in awe. It was modestly furnished, yet tasteful. But compared to her recent years in Germany, it seemed like a palace.

Sabine took a seat on the welcoming chintz sofa as Aunt Mary hurried in and out of the room, setting up teacups and saucers. For the first time in a long time, Sabine felt like she belonged.

Aunt Mary radiated energy, a joy of living Sabine hoped she could aspire to. Now in her mid-forties, Aunt Mary lived life with a passion. She had been divorced for several years and was quite happy with life as a single, cosmopolitan woman.

Sabine stayed with Aunt Mary for several weeks. She treated Sabine like the daughter she had never had, showing her the sights in New York City. They gallivanted around the city exploring all its wonders, from the Statue of Liberty, to Central Park, to the Empire State Building.

What Sabine loved most was wandering through the city's concrete canyons, gawking at the skyscrapers looming above them. Here, the streets were in perpetual shade from the towering buildings. A pleasant breeze drifted in from the bay.

Sabine craned her neck, trying to see the top of the structures. She tried to imagine what it would be like to climb all the way up, higher and higher, until she reached the spire at the summit. The symbolism struck her. Here she stood at the base of skyscrapers, looking way up. It was exactly like how she was in life. She had made it this far, all the way to New York City. Now she had only to climb upward. Just as it would take enormous effort to climb to the top of a skyscraper, it would take tremendous effort to climb to the height of all the promise available in America.

Several happy weeks passed in harmony until Sabine and Aunt Mary had a minor disagreement. The two women stood glaring at each other across the living room.

"But why can't you come with me?" Aunt Mary folded her arms across her chest. She wanted Sabine to come with her to upstate New York for the rest of the summer. She couldn't understand why Sabine wouldn't agree.

Sabine was adamant. "It's not that I don't appreciate your offer," she began, "But it's time I found my own way in the world."

Several hours later, after a tearful discussion, they reached an understanding. Sabine was ready to try her hand at independence, and Aunt Mary grudgingly agreed.

Soon, Sabine landed her first job in America. She became nanny for the infant daughter of Jacob Javits, a New York congressman who was on the fast track to becoming a senator. The take-home pay was one hundred dollars a month, plus room and board. It seemed like a king's ransom to Sabine. These were the days when a hot dog from a street vendor cost fifteen cents, so this was good money. If she was careful, she could easily save almost ninety-five dollars a month.

The instant she laid eyes on baby Joy. Sabine fell in love with her. Joy lived up to her name—she was a happy baby with an engaging smile. Every morning, Sabine would nestle her into her splendid pram, and set out for a walk. It quickly became Sabine's favorite part of the day.

It was on one such morning walk, a few weeks after she had started working for the Javits family, that Sabine was swept with overwhelming homesickness.

As she wheeled Joy about the neighborhood, past stately town houses on tree-lined streets, she caught a snatch of German conversation between two women. They looked like mother and daughter. She only caught the words "synagogue" and "family" before the women hurried past. Immediately, Sabine was transported back to Germany. Her chest ached. Oh, how she missed her family.

It wasn't surprising to hear German in the Javits' neighborhood. There were many German immigrants, and most were Jewish. They were the ones lucky enough to survive Hitler's regime.

Sabine recognized there was something more about this mother and daughter. Perhaps it was how they walked closely together with their arms linked. Or maybe it was the way their laughter lingered behind them on the street. Tears sprang to Sabine's eyes. She sank down onto a nearby park bench, covering her face as salty tears slid down her cheeks.

Still, Sabine was resolute. While she struggled with emotions, her will stayed strong. Her biggest dream had been to move to America. She had worked too hard to give up now.

In addition to frequent homesickness, Sabine had another problem. While she loved baby Joy, she didn't get along with Mrs. Javits. Sabine knew she would have to quit her position with the family.

Her next employment was again as a nanny, this time caring for a set of twins who looked like little cherubs. It was hard work, but Sabine found a place in the life of the family. It helped ease some of her homesickness. The family was fairly well-to-do, and had two houses—one in New York and one in Miami.

Sabine soon realized she wanted to be more than a nanny. Fortunately, her employers allowed her the flexibility to enroll in night school, where she studied hotel management. Each night she drifted off to sleep with a grateful smile. She had only been in America a few months, yet she had already come a long way.

When the family asked her to join them on their next trip to Miami, Sabine was ecstatic. She had already come to love New York City. What was ahead for her in Florida?

7

Where Your Treasure Is, There Your Heart Will Be

Sabine had dropped into paradise. Florida was better than she could have imagined. Palm trees lined the boulevards and beaches, their branches rustling in the gentle breeze. The sky was a vivid blue that dipped right into the rolling ocean.

As the days went on, she felt something unwind deep in her spirit. She hadn't known she was tense until she found herself in this wonderful place where the sun always seemed to shine.

She tried to remember the last time she had felt so happy and secure. To her surprise it had been years—perhaps all the way back to late 1944, when she still lived with her family in Prussia.

Sabine could hardly believe she'd been in America nearly a year. But she didn't consider going back to Europe, even though she still missed her family.

Telephone conversations were costly so they were few and far between. Regular letters from Father became her greatest treasures. When one arrived, she pocketed the letter, retreating to read it as soon as her duties to the family were finished.

She savored the letter in private. Many pages were stained with her tears, and she often thought she could detect dried tear marks from her father, left as he wrote to his only surviving daughter.

Now in palm-strewn Florida, she had more time to reflect, to wonder where she was going with her life, and what her future would hold.

One evening as she took a long walk along the dazzling white beach, she came to a few realizations. While she absolutely loved taking care of the twins, she wanted more.

The sky was just beginning to twinkle with tiny stars when she noticed she wasn't alone. Couples strolled hand in hand along the beach. They walked with their heads close together in quiet conversation.

Sabine sighed. This was a place where romance blossomed. She hadn't had a serious beau yet, and on this night, she found herself gazing wistfully at the couples. *Will I ever meet the right man? What will he be like? And how will I recognize him?*

Before that wish was fulfilled, a stranger gave Sabine a unique opportunity.

The following afternoon, she took the twins for a swim at the Macfadden-Deauville Hotel. It was an upscale hotel, and the pool was quite large. As Sabine played with the girls, she didn't know someone was watching.

At the far end of the pool, a man in a sport shirt and khaki pants sat quietly observing her. It was Warren Freeman, manager of the hotel. Something about this girl drew his attention, He was a powerful man, used to getting exactly what he wanted. He had connections, a man who regularly rubbed shoulders with politicians and movie executives. His business savvy had already benefitted the Macfadden-Deauville Hotel considerably.

Now, as he watched the young woman in the pool, he knew he had to speak to her. She was the right person for the job.

Sabine, of course, was unaware. She didn't notice when he asked an attendant who she was and where she was staying. She didn't know her life was about to change yet again.

She bundled the toddlers in fluffy white towels and hoisted one on each arm. It was amazing how big they were getting. Just as she reached for the gate to leave the pool area, a voice called out.

"Miss Koritke."

She looked back in exasperation to see a fortyish man with thinning fair hair. *Couldn't he see she was in a hurry?* The children were heavy, and by now, they had begun to cry and fuss.

Still, she found her manners. "Yes, sir?" It didn't occur to her to wonder how this professional looking person knew her name.

He smiled. "I am Warren Freeman, manager of this hotel." He said it as if his name should mean something to her.

Sabine blushed. "I'm sorry we used your pool when we're not paying guests, sir. The receptionist in the lobby said it was okay."

The man waved off her apology. "Never mind," he said. "I have a business proposition I'd like to discuss with you."

Sabine just stood there looking at him.

He continued, "Would you allow me to take you to dinner tonight to discuss it?"

Still holding the crying twins, Sabine was taken aback. *Who is this guy?*

"What kind of business proposition?" she asked guardedly.

The man smiled. "It's all very legitimate, I assure you. I know the family you work for. Ask them. They'll vouch for me."

Sabine was flustered. If this man really was a friend of the family, she couldn't risk insulting him. And he was nice enough. A sense of power and excitement radiated from him. Something told her if she met him for dinner, her life would never be the same.

"Alright, I can meet you for dinner."

Warren Freeman's face lit up like a little boy in the toy store.

Once she arrived back with the twins, she mentioned the bizarre encounter to her employers.

"Warren Freeman has a business proposition for you?" the father exclaimed. He was a journalist and would have loved a dinner with Warren Freeman.

"So he's legitimate," Sabine asked, "and trustworthy?"

"Absolutely."

Her boss said nothing more. He guessed that Sabine's days as their nanny were numbered.

A few hours later, Sabine found herself standing nervously in the lobby of the Macfadden-Deauville Hotel. She wore her best outfit, a peach colored shirtwaist with turned up collar and cuffed sleeves. Still she felt underdressed when she saw the hotel's crystal chandeliers spaced along the soaring ceiling.

Her fears were soon put to ease, however, as Warren Freeman approached her with a wide smile.

"My dear, you look lovely tonight," he reached out and gently brought her cool hand to his lips.

The evening took off from there, and within minutes, Sabine

41

and Warren were chatting comfortably. He turned out to be a charming man. Sabine could see why he was successful.

Over dinner that night, Sabine knew she had made a friend. She didn't feel anything romantic. But she knew instinctively they would have an agreeable friendship, the kind they could both rely on.

After eating their Chateaubriand, the talk turned to business. Warren's gaze turned serious. "I have a fabulous opportunity for you, Sabine." He laid his crisp linen napkin aside.

Sabine sipped a fine burgundy. Whatever he was about to suggest would be good.

"I would like to offer you a position in this hotel, assisting my wife to make sure our guests are cared for."

Sabine was surprised. The Macfadden-Deauville Hotel and Casino catered to the rich and famous–people like Sammy Davis, Jr., Frank Sinatra, and Dean Martin. Their clientele demanded seamless, expert service. It was a terrific opportunity.

"But, why are you offering me this?" she asked.

"It's something about you, sweet Sabine. I'm a good judge of people." Warren smiled. "You are a captivating contradiction of innocence and poise. The moment I saw you, I knew you'd go far."

They spent the rest of the evening in pleasant conversation. By evening's end, Sabine knew this was too good to pass up. Her job would be to meet the needs of the hotel's guests, the cream of American society. She would greet them, pamper them, and fulfill every whim and fancy. She would basically ensure their experience at the Macfadden-Deauville lived up to the luxury the hotel was known for. And Sabine thought the pay was excellent–two hundred dollars a month. She had come a long way from sharing a room with her family in someone else's house, or sleeping in the barn of a kind farmer's wife.

On her way home that night, she slipped off her pumps and walked along the soft sandy beach. Mr. Freeman had offered to walk her home but she wanted to be alone. She needed time to think.

The moon was a large pearl, its light dancing across the black ocean. A slight breeze teased Sabine's hair as she stood watching the waves ripple in. Her heart felt light and eager. Overnight, her world had turned from mere survival to one full of promise. She knew she was on a fast track to the success she had craved. Soon, she'd be surrounded by rich, famous, beautiful people.

In the past, people told her she was beautiful, but she dismissed it as empty flattery. Tonight she actually felt pretty. She had seen it in the way Warren Freeman looked at her. It was intoxicating.

She let her dreams drift to the future. Meeting Mr. Freeman had sprung open a treasure chest of wishes, long packed away. Now she wondered, *Will I meet someone and fall in love? And what if my future husband turns out to be one of the hotel's wealthy guests?*

She allowed herself a secret smile. How wonderful to be married, to truly belong to someone who loved and cared for her. She knew what kind of man she wanted. He had to be honest, a hard worker, a man with principles. In short, a man like her father. *And if he happens to carry the wealth of untold millions... well, who am I to complain?*

8

A Friend Loves at all Times

S he returned to her employers' home, floating on air.
Much later that night she woke with panic and a knot in her stomach. *Can I really serve wealthy, famous people? At one of the best hotels in Miami?* She twisted on her bed and tried to put it out of her mind. It was no use. She wasn't afraid of office work, or managing resources. It was the people part—moving among these high society types with confidence. She had always been a little shy, and often felt an embarrassing blush creep up her cheeks when talking to strangers.

Now she had agreed to take a position that hinged on her ability to interact with important people. All day long! *What have I gotten myself into?*

She lay there worrying for several hours. But by the time her alarm clock jangled, she had made up her mind. She had to do this. Backing out had never been her style, and certainly not now, when she was about to cross a threshold to a new life.

Within a few days her fears evaporated. She fit easily into her new role, and with each successful day, her confidence grew. The guests found her charming, with her bright smile and lilting European accent. She was the perfect hostess, meeting the needs of each guest in a way that reminded them how special they were.

Meanwhile, she had said goodbye to her employers and hugged the twins one last time. She moved to a small apartment not far from the hotel.

Soon after, Sabine met a young French girl around her own age, sitting alone in the hotel's restaurant. "Hello, I'm Janine," she smiled at Sabine with an impish grin. Her raven hair curled around a face that held flashing black eyes. Sabine liked her immediately.

At that moment, the two became friends. It wasn't just that they were both recent immigrants to the United States. They also viewed the world in a similar fashion and laughed at the same jokes.

Janine had little to laugh about, though. Sabine learned her bright smile hid a desperately unhappy young woman. Janine had just come off a terrible divorce which followed an even worse marriage. She married young, to an American pilot she met while working as a stewardess. Shortly after the wedding, she discovered he was prone to extramarital affairs.

"He had about as many affairs as flights," she said. The ink was barely dry on their divorce papers, and yet, she confided to Sabine, "Part of me still loves him." Her voice broke. "I've been so alone. I miss him terribly."

Her husband had left her virtually penniless. Not knowing where to go, she had taken a room at the Macfadden-Deauville Hotel. She knew it was foolish to stay at such an expensive place. But she and her husband had stayed there and it was the only place that was familiar

Janine's brown eyes filled with tears. "I have only enough money to stay the weekend. I don't know where I'll go on Monday."

Sabine looked carefully at the petite girl. Then she made an uncharacteristic snap decision. "Why don't you move in with me?"

Janine's money problem was solved just as easily. Sabine had an idea. "Wait here," she said to Janine.

She returned moments later with Warren Freeman. One look at Janine was all Warren Freeman needed. Despite her current distress, she had a casual elegance that complemented her dark complexion and foreign beauty. After a few questions, he could tell she was quite intelligent. She could also speak several languages fluently. He hired her on the spot.

And so, the two young women embarked on an adventure—at work, and as roommates.

With their striking good looks and European charm, they were soon immersed in Miami's social scene. Sabine especially loved the private parties held in villas on the outskirts of the city.

The parties were luxurious events with select guests. Within weeks, the two were welcomed within these circles. Sabine was making up for her lost youth during the war years. She couldn't have felt further from the fear and despair that surrounded her in Germany..

The opulent mansions amazed her. Giant wrought iron gates swung open to reveal virtual castles. Most were built beside the ocean. Cocktail parties at sunset were stunning as an orange Florida sun sank into the molten sea.

The buffets were always lavish, as if the goal was to surpass previous parties. Sabine liked to stroll the estate grounds arm in arm with a friend, taking in gardens overflowing with red, magenta, lavender, and yellow blossoms on exotic plants. She admired the full-sized tennis courts, the swimming pools, the splashing fountains—all luxuries she hoped to have one day.

At one such party, Sabine found herself with champagne glass in hand, standing on a large veranda overlooking the sea. The waves rolled in, crashing with white foam. The view was glorious.

Then she turned and looked at a large cage on the veranda. She could hardly believe it. In an evident attempt to "best" their millionaire friends, the hosts had a fully grown ape in a cage. As Sabine studied the animal's mournful eyes, he was like a metaphor. For the first time she realized people could live in the midst of all this wealth and not be free.

And yet, she and Janine continued to regularly attend the parties, living the high life. With some variation, the same people attended every party. Of course, Warren Freeman was always invited. He showed mild amusement that his two "European Ladies" had rapidly climbed the social ladder. Sabine and Janine were on every invitation list.

Their new American friends found them enchanting. Women admired their grace, and men were entranced by their beauty. Sabine and Janine quickly learned the fine art of flirtation, wrapping men around their well-manicured fingers.

Both girls knew their popularity was superficial. They were valued because they were exotic. No one had real interest in them. High society showed them off in a kind of exhibition, something to make their parties more interesting. For some reason, Sabine remembered the ape in the cage.

9

There is Nothing Better than to Enjoy One's Work

S abine wasn't interested in the men they met. There was always something wrong with them. Some talked about themselves too much–vain blowhards Others drank endless amounts, always staying just sober enough for society. Sabine and Janine often returned to their apartment laughing over the latest clumsy advance of a man.

The two girls had one simple rule: They came to a party together and they went home together. They declined all offers to take a sociable chat to a more intimate level.

One night before going to bed, Sabine stood looking at herself in the little mirror above the bathroom sink. So many had said she was beautiful. Maybe she was. Wherever she went, heads turned.

Sabine pulled a brush through her chestnut hair. She thought, *I hate my looks. I want people to love me for who I really am.* To her surprise, salty tears welled up and spilled down her cheeks. *I want something more, but I don't know what it is!*

Warren Freeman wouldn't have recognized Sabine's yearning. He was proud of her reception by Miami's elite. After all, he was the one who "discovered" her in the first place. And he had even greater plans in mind. He knew her talents could take her farther than the Macfadden-Deauville, as fine an establishment as it was.

One quiet afternoon, Sabine was sitting in the garden of the hotel, enjoying her lunch break. Flowers bloomed all around her and she breathed in their heady perfume.

"Sabine?"

She looked up to see Warren Freeman. He sat down beside her at a glass-topped wicker table. The garden waiter appeared and served him a frosty glass of Perrier.

"I've been impressed with your work at the hotel," Freeman began. "You are a capable woman."

Sabine beamed.

"I have a new opportunity. As you know, I have business dealings with the Quarterdeck Club."

Sabine nodded. Warren had invited her a few times to the exclusive yacht club.

"I am looking for a new hostess there. I hope you'll consider it."

Sabine's heart began a tap dance. Freeman was offering a big advancement in her career. "That sounds exciting. What would my duties be?"

Warren grinned his self-assured smile. "You'll see."

Sabine didn't dare ask anything else. Even though she had mastered the art of exuding confidence, she was still intimidated by anyone in authority. Even someone she had known as long as Warren Freeman.

After a moment, Warren laughed. "Hey, I'll tell you this

49

much. It'll get very, very interesting."

He raised his glass to her in a toast, then went back inside the hotel.

Two days later Sabine began working at the Quarterdeck Club. From the moment she stepped out of the launch, she loved the place.

The Quarterdeck Club was perched in Biscayne Bay, and was only accessible by boat. Yachts filled the slips of its marina. Guests could dock for a couple of hours, or sometimes days, before departing for destinations in the Caribbean, out in the Atlantic, or over to the Gulf of Mexico.

The club itself was a dazzling white structure, anchored on posts, sitting low over peacock blue water. A broad terrace wrapped around it, inviting guests to lounge in its shade and enjoy a gorgeous view in all directions. On one side, the ocean offered an endless horizon. On the other, Miami's coast with its boardwalks and beaches stretched lazily in the sunshine.

Warren pointed out the cozy rooms for overnight guests, which sported round portholes instead of windows, opened to sea breezes. But when they walked into the nautical-style cocktail lounge, Sabine could hardly believe her eyes. A fishing hatch was placed directly beside the bar! The hatch was open, revealing the ocean beneath. Guests sat there fishing while enjoying their cocktails.

Within a few days, Sabine realized the Quarterdeck Club was a whole new level of luxury. The first time she received a tip from a client she thought she would faint. So much money! The customers were generous, the work was interesting, and the atmosphere proved even more exclusive than the Macfadden-Deauville. Sabine's days filled with summer sun, and the sons of rich parents.

When the girls returned to their apartment after another extravagant soiree, Janine turned to Sabine with a sad look in her dark eyes.

"I've made a decision. I'm moving back home to my family in France."

Sabine felt a dull ache. She had said too many goodbyes in her young life. The days sped by as Janine got ready to leave. Each night, the young women stayed up late, talking and crying. Finally, on the morning of Janine's departure, they shared a tearful farewell. Sabine wondered if she would ever see her friend again.

She left for work that morning with a heavy heart. She decided to throw herself into her work. Her position at the yacht club was as fulfilling as Warren Freeman had promised. In addition to serving needs of the guests, Sabine took the launch to the mainland every Friday. She returned with colorful baskets filled with groceries and supplies. Soon the owner also made Sabine responsible for the cash register. She even tended bar occasionally, but that was the only job she didn't enjoy.

Working in the open air was better, with the fresh breeze ruffling her hair and the Florida sun warming her face. One afternoon, she painted the deck a cheery yellow.

It was hard to remember what life had been like before. Miami socialites still invited her to their grand parties, but they weren't the same without Janine.

Sabine eventually gave up her apartment, choosing to live at the Quarterdeck Club. Her little room on the ocean became a cozy sanctuary that met her needs perfectly.

Sometimes when her duties were finished, she borrowed a small boat and slipped out to sea. Surrounded only by water, she sat quietly as the boat bobbed on the waves. Life in Germany, particularly the bombing and flames of Dresden and Dessau, seemed to have happened on another planet.

Not that no danger lurked here. Sharks showed up on a regular basis. Sabine often looked out her porthole and saw fins slicing through the water. How unsettling to think that six feet below her, sharks swam by as she lay sleeping!

Yet, if there existed one place in the world where heaven kissed the earth, it was here. It was more than the warm, clear water, the glistening coastline, the sleek yachts, or even the tanned, wealthy, mostly male guests who showered attention on her. Life was so simple here–and yet so very rich.

She also basked in the knowledge of Warren Freeman's trust. Because of the strong work ethic of her Prussian family, she was a model employee. Sabine always did everything to perfection.

After several months, they promoted her to manager. In addition to making sure everything ran smoothly, she was to make sure the guests were happy, to chat and mingle with them.

Sabine's closest friend at the club was the bartender, Freddy. She called him "Cowboy," while his nickname for her was "Sweet Sabine." Soon the club regulars also began calling her that.

This should have been the happiest time of her life. But one day, while out on the ocean in the little boat, her mind turned to unsettling things. *What am I doing with my life? How long can I stay here, providing novelty for people who have too much of everything? Will I ever marry?*

She took hold of the oars and began to row back to the club. *When I do marry,* she vowed, *he must be a man of wealth, a man with class.*

By now, she was quite expert at flirting–but always in a subtle way that left men wanting more. With a simple look she could have nearly any man eating out of her hand.

The only damper was when another letter arrived from her father back in Germany. In letter after letter, he warned of the dangers of excess wealth, and the superficial life of the upper class. Over and over, his letters to his only daughter stressed faithfulness, diligence, truthfulness, and loyalty—principles he had taught her long ago. She loved him, but his letters were becoming annoying. He was as if he were watching her from thousands of miles away.

For awhile, Sabine toned down her charismatic personality, just a bit. But life at the club proved too intoxicating. Even Father's most dire warnings couldn't distract her for long.

Just being around wealthy, famous people was worth an occasional twinge of conscience. People such as hotel magnate, Conrad Hilton, and bandleader, Benny Goodman, frequented the club. Actors, politicians, and businessmen jostled their way in front of photographers' lenses, eager to be seen in the society pages.

Sabine noticed that very little shocked her anymore. No matter what went on in the bar, in the rooms, or in the yachts tied alongside, the Quarterdeck Club kept things discreet. Sabine was amazed that some of the more sordid behavior didn't find its way into the tabloids.

Presidents and CEOs of large companies frequented the club, along with the heads of major airlines. Sabine watched as Freddy poured drink after drink. She never learned to stomach the ones who got more and more inebriated. As their alcohol levels rose, they disgusted her.

One man struck her as different. He walked in on a windy, rainy night when the club was nearly deserted. He came with one of the club regulars, a Cuban bon vivant named Bebe Rebozo. As Sabine took their dripping trench coats, she watched the newcomer.

10

He Has Brought Down Rulers from Their Thrones

There's something special about him, Sabine thought as she escorted Rebozo and the new man into the club. He was good looking, with dark hair. She guessed he was in his forties.

"We were going fishing," Rebozo said with a grimace. "Then this squall blew in. Good thing we weren't too far from the club."

Leading the men to the bar, Sabine asked Bebe's friend, "Do you have a special request, Mister…?"

"Call me Richard," he said with a gentle smile.

As she turned to leave them, he said, "Would you care to sit with us, miss?"

Sabine considered. The club was nearly empty. Why not enjoy their company? She settled onto a bar stool.

As Freddy poured drinks for the men and a mineral water for her, she studied the new guest. Richard was dressed in casual tropical clothes that were still tasteful. By now, Sabine was pretty good at sizing up men. And Richard impressed her. His quiet reserve was especially appealing. He didn't say one word too many, and gave no sign of the bragging that was common in the club. And yet he was friendly and laughed easily. He seemed genuinely interested in getting to know Sabine.

"You're not an American, are you?" It was more a statement than a question.

"No, I'm not. I've only worked two years in the States."

"From Germany?"

Sabine nodded yes. Her accent was always a dead giveaway. Most guests stopped there, not sure what to say. After all, it wasn't that long since Americans were at war with Germans.

However, Richard wasn't at loss for words. He leaned forward, his dark eyes fixed intently on her. He began to ask question after question. Why had she left Germany? What part of the country was she from? And most important, how had she survived during the war?

The storm continued outside, and a driving rain pelted the roof as they talked late into the night. For the first time, Sabine had found someone who wanted to know about her life in Germany. As the hours went by, she opened up to this dark stranger, telling him the terrors of Dresden, and Dessau. And still, Richard acted interested. She told him about her father and about the *Wilhelm Gustloff* sinking, the brutalities of the Russian occupation force, and her work in the American officers' club in *Günzburg*.

Then Richard asked, "What about Hitler? What did the *Führer* mean to you?"

Sabine took her time answering. Something about this man drew out her innermost thoughts. She told about her father's reaction to the BBC news on that night, long ago. She even revealed her secret admiration of Hitler, and then her profound disillusionment.

She had never met an American who was so interested in Germany, and who knew so much about her homeland. She decided that he must be very educated.

Despite Sabine's personal revelations, she learned very little about Richard himself. He said he was a lawyer, born in Yorba Linda, California. She thought there was more to his story, but he didn't elaborate. From some of his comments, she picked up that he served in the navy during the war.

One thing he was quite open about: He hated communism. Richard was genuinely moved when she told how Marxism had taken over East Germany—East Prussia, as she knew it. He showed sympathy for the way communism had strangled her country. "What a tragedy," he repeated again and again.

The dark, rainy hours swept by. When they went to their separate rooms, it was almost morning. As Sabine drifted into a peaceful sleep, she didn't have a clue whom she had spent several hours with, sharing her life story.

Several nights later, Bebe Rebozo told her who her companion was on that rainy night. The name Richard Nixon didn't mean anything, but when Bebe told her he was a U.S. senator from California, her face blanched.

Rebozo crowed with laughter, then offered to buy her a drink.

A few years later, Sabine watched on TV as Nixon was sworn in as the thirty-seventh president of the United States. If she had known his true identity, she wouldn't have felt so free to spend hours, telling him all about herself.

Not long after her encounter with Richard Nixon, Sabine met another man who impressed her. However, this was a meeting that would change her life.

*****

He introduced himself as Clifford Ball. "But everyone calls me Cliff," he said.

She welcomed him into the Quarterdeck Club, casting a quick glance at his enormous yacht at the marina.

Over time Cliff became a regular guest at the club. She learned he hadn't been content to be the wealthy heir of an established family. He had rapidly climbed the ladder of fortune himself.

Every time he came to the club, Cliff's eyes searched for Sabine.

As for her, she thought he was a bit old at thirty-two. And he was more serious than most of the lighthearted sons of the wealthy. But still, there was something about him.

His hair had already started to gray, and he carried himself with dignity and confidence. By all appearances, he was a man with money and time to enjoy his fancy yacht with his favorite drink in hand.

What made him stand out was his interest in Sabine. From the moment he arrived at the club, he sent boyish glances her way. He took every opportunity to lavish compliments on her. But it was his helpfulness that really got her attention.

Cliff started going along on her shopping trips to the mainland. Each Friday they set out, using his Cadillac to go from store to store. Sabine carried her list of what was needed for the week—fruits and vegetables, nails and screws for the workshop, fabric to decorate the bar. Cliff plodded along, helping to carry her purchases. Sabine found herself strangely annoyed by this man who never offered his opinions on anything, even on which stores to go to. Instead, he left every decision to her.

She told herself, *I be grateful for his help. Who else gets driven around in a shiny new Cadillac to shop?*

Cliff wasn't the only one with eyes for Sabine. Eurith was the son of a former governor of Georgia. He learned about her Friday shopping trips and said, "Whenever you need help, just let me know and I'll send my chauffeur."

Sabine found the idea of a chauffeur fairly exciting. One Friday afternoon, Cliff was unable to go with her, so she took Eurith up on his offer.

As her launch pulled up to the dock, she could see the long, black limousine waiting. She slid into the front seat beside the chauffeur, a large black man resplendent in a uniform with shiny buttons.

An embarrassed silence filled the limo.

The chauffeur said quietly, "It's customary for a lady to sit in the back seat, not up front with the chauffeur."

The afternoon went downhill from there. Sabine found herself missing Cliff and their uncomplicated shopping experiences.

The next week, she made more of an effort to appreciate Cliff. She was surprised to learn he was quite frugal, despite the family fortune. But while he dabbled in various enterprises, he was first and foremost the son of a very wealthy man.

He lived in one of his parents' large houses in Miami, while his parents spent most of their time in Philadelphia. When Cliff spoke of his parents, his voice took on a reverent tone. He had never rebelled against them, even as a youth. Why should he? After all, they gave him everything he wanted. He was content with his life.

The only part of him that Sabine found thrilling was his

money. Other than that, he was boring. Still, she was excited to have such an ardent admirer. And he definitely admired her. His eyes were always on her, love written all over his face.

One afternoon as they piled their purchases into his Cadillac, Sabine sensed he was trying to say something. Finally, he jammed his hands in his pockets and said in a rush, "Would you have dinner with me tonight?"

Sabine was startled. They had never gone on a real date. But what was the harm of a simple dinner?

She agreed.

The evening turned out to be anything but simple. Cliff took her to one of the fanciest restaurants in Miami. They sat at a table draped in white linen, and feasted on one delicacy after another. Sabine nibbled at the fish course and it melted in her mouth. She sipped white sparkling wine from a slim crystal flute. Everything about this evening was magical.

She smiled at Cliff and thought, *A millionaire is sitting across from me! He has chosen me and me alone to spend the evening with.*

A blissful feeling rose inside her. She decided Cliff wasn't boring. He wasn't handsome in the classic sense of the word, but he did maintain a trim figure. And he could be fun. She already knew that from the Quarterdeck Club. Cliff was shy until he had one or two drinks in him. Then he really came out of his shell.

One night he had pretended to be the waiter. He folded his napkin, draped it over his right arm, and sashayed from table to table. The entire room erupted in laughter. Sabine thought her sides would split in two.

She put knife and fork into her filet mignon and it cut like butter. Yes, this man across from her could be fun. He enjoyed life and got a lot of pleasure from his expensive toys. In addition to his yacht, he liked to skim about Biscayne Bay in his speedboat. Sabine smiled as she thought, *If I'm not completely in love with him, I sure don't mind his lifestyle!*

He looked across the table, lifted his glass toward her, and smiled. Sabine thought, *Maybe I'm already in love with him. Have I been in love with him all along and not realized it?*

11

Charm is Deceptive and Beauty is Fleeting

A ll in all, their first date had gone very well. Sabine was especially impressed when they left the restaurant without anyone presenting them a bill. Men like Cliff could pay with their good name.

Sabine settled into his Cadillac and they swept past the pastel Art Deco buildings and swaying palm trees of Miami. When he parked at the dock where his speedboat waited to take her back to the Quarterdeck Club, he made no move to get out of the car. Instead, he reached across and gently took her hand.

He smiled at Sabine, looking like a bashful boy. Reaching inside his jacket, he pulled out a small black box.

She noticed his hands were trembling. She caught her breath.

Cliff smiled, looking deep into her eyes. "Will you marry me, Sabine?" He opened the box and she saw a flash of fire. It was a ring with the biggest diamond she'd ever seen.

Sabine was dumbfounded. Her brain couldn't form a sentence. She hadn't dreamed that Cliff had been planning this. And on their first date! Inside her head a million warning bells clanged like crazy, and she couldn't utter a word.

She managed a strangled, "Cliff?"

He misunderstood and replied softly, "Sabine…."

She regained her speech. "I can't accept this. I can't say yes. Not now. It's… too fast." She tried to ignore the hurt that sprang to his eyes.

Cliff pressed his lips together and sighed deeply. "Of course," he said. He looked down at the box and muttered more to himself than to her, "This ring cost me seven thousand dollars!"

Sabine remained firm, even when offered such an extravagant ring. Her mind flashed to her father in Germany. *If he could see me now, he'd be so proud.*

"Did you think you could buy me?" she asked.

Cliff looked puzzled. She knew he was used to getting whatever he wanted, no matter the cost. And now, he wanted her.

Sabine laid her hand on his, still holding the jewelry box. "I'm sorry, Cliff. I want to be absolutely certain. When I marry, I want to stay married. I just need some time."

In the days following Cliff's surprise proposal, Sabine spent many sleepless nights. Had she made the right decision? She was wracked with uncertainty. She knew Cliff's proposal still stood. She only had to say the word and she would become Mrs. Clifford Ball. But… was that what she wanted? Would she be happy, married to Cliff?

One night she woke with a start. Although she still didn't know what to do about Cliff's proposal, she was absolutely clear about one thing. She wanted to go home—to Europe.

It had been more than two years since she'd arrived in America. Her spirit yearned for her family and her dear friend.

She wanted their advice. And perhaps a little distance would help her make up her mind.

She had never taken time off, so it was easy to ask for a short leave of absence. She planned to visit Janine in Paris, then travel on to Germany. The first part of the trip would be easier than the last. While she was eager for her father's advice, she also feared it. From his many letters, she knew he didn't exactly approve of her lifestyle, nor of her ambitions to marry a rich man.

Janine met Sabine's ship at Le Havre. The two hugged each other and cried. Soon they were lounging on Janine's sofa in her small Paris apartment, drinking champagne.

"I want to ask your advice about something," Sabine said.

"You know I can always give advice," the French girl said, laughing.

"Someone has asked me to marry him...."

"Wow! I knew you'd catch a rich bachelor at the Quarterdeck Club." Janine lifted her champagne glass. "We've got to drink to this."

They clinked their glasses together.

Sabine smiled, then suddenly serious, put her glass down on the coffee table. "I really don't know what to do. I can't help but wonder.... Is he the right one?"

Janine studied her friend, then said, "When your dream begins to come true, you shouldn't stand in its way."

For the rest of her time in Paris, Janine's words resonated with Sabine. The two talked into the wee hours of the morning, telling stories punctuated with lots of laughter, and even spontaneous hugs.

The highlight was an evening spent in a Parisian nightclub. They danced and flirted the night away, like they used to do in Miami's high society. But here, the atmosphere was small and intimate.

"More champagne?" asked their waitress, an attentive young woman wearing a white apron.

"Thank you! Not for the moment," Sabine answered. At ten dollars a flask, it was time to switch to mineral water.

"Okay," Janine leaned back, "I want to hear all about the Quarterdeck Club."

Sabine told of recent adventures, including her night talking with Richard Nixon. Janine had read about him in the papers.

Janine took in her breath sharply. She whispered, "You won't believe who just came in. It's the Shah!"

She raised her left eyebrow and nodded in the direction of a table across the club.

Sabine turned as subtly as possible and saw a handsome man with a square jaw and coal black hair. He was wearing an exquisitely tailored dark suit. Even seated, he made an imposing figure. Just then he looked right at her. Sabine turned back quickly.

"Uh oh, he saw us looking at him!" She giggled.

Janine kept looking over Sabine's shoulder. "Hey, he's nodding to us!" she whispered.

Sabine sat stiffly in her chair, not daring to turn around again.

"Yes, he's definitely smiling at us. Turn around and give him that Sweet Sabine smile!"

"I'll do no such thing," Sabine hissed. But she couldn't resist sneaking another peek. It was true! The dapper man from the Middle East was grinning broadly at them. Suddenly, he stood up.

"He's coming over!" Janine squealed.

The next thing Sabine knew, she was looking up into the man's large brown eyes.

"May I trouble you for this dance?" he asked in perfect English.

Sabine couldn't resist. He offered his arm and led her smoothly to the dance floor. She threw a look back at Janine, who looked vastly amused.

The Shah—or whoever he was—turned out to be an excellent dancer. As they spun about the dance floor, Sabine noted his thick eyebrows and well-defined facial features. He was truly a good-looking man.

Glasses of champagne, a mysterious, handsome dance partner…. Life doesn't get any better than this. Sabine decided. *From now on, I'll see what opportunities arise, then dance my way through life.*

12

Wide is the Gate and Broad is the Road that Leads to Destruction

After their dance, the man invited them to his table. As they sat down, Janine squeezed Sabine's hand. What a thrilling evening!

"Ladies, it's a pleasure to make your acquaintance," said their host gallantly, his kind eyes twinkling. "May I order you something to drink?"

Sabine had no objection. They spent the next several hours dancing, laughing, and drinking vast amounts of champagne. Their conversation went no further than small talk. They certainly didn't learn much about the dark, handsome man. Strictly speaking, they learned nothing, not even his name. Instead, they schmoozed about a wide variety of unimportant things. Most of all, they laughed and had fun.

It was almost four in the morning when the waitress politely signaled that the club was closing and it was time for them to pay.

Sabine and Janine settled back as the excitement of the evening drained away. Then to their shock, their friendly, obviously wealthy companion took out his wallet and carefully paid for his own drinks.

The waitress turned toward the young women. Sabine looked down at the check and swallowed. It was a huge amount. The two girls stared at each other in disbelief. Their new friend expected them to pay for their own drinks. He was not the gentleman they had thought.

Sabine's disbelief changed to fierce anger. She yanked some francs from her handbag and threw them onto the table.
They left the nightclub in stony silence. The waitress helped them hail a taxi. Sabine was even more irritated when the man got into the taxi with them! Was he expecting them to pay his fare as well?

As the cab pulled up in front of Janine's apartment, the man spoke. "Would you grant me the great pleasure tomorrow morning," he paused dramatically, "of having breakfast with me? I'd gladly invite you to my hotel."

Without hesitation or even asking Janine, Sabine spit out, "No, thank you!" The girls shut the door of the taxi behind them and left without saying goodbye.

"Goodbye and good riddance!" Sabine muttered as they charged up the stairs to Janine's apartment.

The next morning, Sabine came into the kitchen. Janine had just brought in the morning paper, still rubbing sleep from her eyes. Then Sabine heard a loud gasp.

Janine showed her the newspaper without saying a word. There, plastered on the front page, was a photo of the man who had made them pay for their own drinks the night before. Below the photo it read, "Mohammad Reza Pahlavi, the Shah of Iran in Paris."

Sabine and Janine's mouths dropped open. Their dancing

and drinking companion, the man whose invitation Sabine loudly spurned, was none other than the reigning Imperial Majesty of Iran.

They spent the morning in silence. Finally, Sabine said, "Well, I wasn't born to be a Persian empress anyway!"

Several days, later, Sabine boarded a train for Dusseldorf. As she rode through the summer countryside, she saw signs of peace and prosperity. Farmers had planted their fields, and in the towns they passed, Sabine noticed new buildings and repairs to old ones. It was hard to remember the horrors of war.

As her train chugged eastward, Sabine's feelings were torn. After two years away, she was going to see Father, Mother, and Hans—now a teenager. Ella had married and moved away. It would be so good to see her family. But Sabine knew this was no longer home. She was here for a visit, nothing more. Her home was Florida.

At this point she couldn't say whether she would live as Miss Sabine Koritke in the Quarterdeck Club, or in a villa as Mrs. Clifford Ball. But she would have to make a decision soon.

As the train pulled into Dusseldorf Station, her family was waiting, lined up on the platform. She grabbed her bags and flew off the train, into the arms of Father. Mother and Hans were there, too. Sabine couldn't believe how tall Hans had grown.

The visit flew by all too fast. Over a dinner of beef roulade, boiled potatoes, and Mother's wonderful brown gravy, Sabine told stories of her new life in America. Hans shot question after question. He seemed proud of his big sister.

She told how she had gone from being a nanny to becoming manager of the Quarterdeck Club. However, the longer

Sabine raved about the Miami mansions, the lavish parties, the exclusive clientele of the club, and their expensive yachts, the heavier Father's silence grew.

Finally, she asked, "Why are you so quiet, Father?"

"People with values shun those millionaire playgrounds," he replied with a pained expression.

Sabine and the others listened quietly as Father spoke softly for quite a long time, praising a life lived simply, full of truthfulness and honesty.

"You won't find that with these puffed-up folks," he said, his hands shaking. "Not these rich people who only live to flaunt their wealth."

Sabine and her mother took the dishes into the kitchen, returning with cups of coffee. Because she knew Father so well, she realized those words had come straight from his heart. He also spoke with much love. He hated rebuking any of his children.

Sabine took a sip of coffee, then plunged ahead, telling them about Cliff, his life of privilege, and even his marriage proposal. But after she read Father's face, she left out the part about the seven-thousand-dollar ring. She tried to explain how wonderful it was, being around Cliff who floated through life. "It's so fantastic, Father!"

He didn't reply. He just sat there, full of Prussian dignity. However, his face said everything.

Her coffee grew cold as she tried to explain what a great man Cliff was. And somehow, the more Sabine tried to convince Father, the more her own mind was made up. She remembered Paris, how she wanted to dance through life. She wanted to have fun—a lot of fun! What was wrong with that?

It was futile, trying to convince Father. Still, she prattled on until he interrupted her, looking deeply into her eyes. "Good heavens, girl, be honest with yourself!"

Sabine stopped, not saying another word.

The rest of her time in Germany passed in a blur. She and Father never spoke of Cliff again, but she carried the burden of his disapproval in her heart.

Before she knew it, she was back on a ship headed for America. On the last day of the voyage she stood at the ship's rail, watching the choppy waves of the Atlantic. In only a few hours, she would see the upraised arm of the Statue of Liberty. Europe lay behind her, America before her.

So much had changed since the first time she sailed into a U.S. harbor. Her life couldn't be more different. She felt like an American now, and the ship was bringing her home.

She leaned over the railing, staring down at the dark blue water. The sea always impressed her with its unfathomable depths. She tried to forget her father's words, but they continued to sear her soul. "Seek people with true values. And make no compromise!"

13

Unless the Lord Builds the House, the Builders Labor in Vain

Sabine stepped inside the entryway of the Ball mansion. She suddenly felt very small and insignificant. Though she had attended many parties in fancy villas, this was enormous. This was the first time the Ball family had invited Sabine to their home.

As Cliff gave her a tour of the mansion, her mouth dropped open in amazement. If she had counted correctly, it had nine fully furnished bathrooms. Six featured giant chandeliers. Chandeliers in the bathrooms!

There were eight bedrooms, many opening into full suites. Every single bedroom could easily engulf the little apartment she had rented in Miami. In addition to the bedroom suites, there were numerous dining and living rooms, parlors, lounges, and a large swimming pool beside one of their sumptuous gardens.

"Naturally," Cliff declared offhandedly as they continued their tour, "We require many servants." She lost count of the household staff who passed by in respectful silence. Cliff said they lived in their own quarters in the back.

The mansion was comparable to the grand manors that dotted the landscape of her childhood. But Sabine saw the difference. German castles and estates were masterfully understated inside. But the Ball home was flashy, with gaudy colors and over-sized furniture. Many rooms seemed to scream as she entered. She realized it must be the mark of Cliff's mother.

As if on cue, Mrs. Ball made an appearance.

"Welcome, Sabine. Am I pronouncing your name right?" Mrs. Ball reached to take her hand.

Although she welcomed Sabine, Mrs. Ball soon showed herself to be loud and shrill, and more than a little nervous. Still, she was the perfect hostess, with an appropriate smile that never wavered. Cliff had already told her his mother's entire life consisted of parties, both throwing them and attending those of others. Sabine tried to forget Father's words about the idle rich.

She noticed Mrs. Ball was wearing what looked like a very expensive necklace, sparkling with diamonds.

"That's a handsome piece of jewelry, Mrs. Ball."

"Of course, I only wear a duplicate–a custom-made design, dear," Mrs. Ball tittered as she fingered the necklace. "The original stays locked away in the safe."

What a paradox, thought Sabine. *The rich can afford fabulous jewelry, yet they wear fake necklaces! Will I ever understand Cliff's world?*

As Cliff completed his extensive tour of their home, Sabine was in a daze. She had known he was wealthy, but she had never fathomed how wealthy. What had it been like for a little boy growing up in this palace?

Cliff told her his father was rarely home because of business responsibilities.

No wonder he was always gone, being married to your mother, Sabine nearly said aloud. Then she pushed aside that judgmental thought. *I will respect Cliff's parents,* she decided, *just like I respect mine.*

Anyway, despite any failings as a parent, Cliff's father was enormously successful in business. *Cliff will never have to work a day in his life,* Sabine thought. Then she quickly banished that idea, too. She mustn't think about Cliff lacking ambition. It wasn't his fault his parents made everything so easy. Besides, his mother probably squelched any motivation Cliff had. No wonder he drifted through life. He was amiable, charming, and easygoing. She could love this man. And if not, surely his wealth would make up for the emptiness in her heart.

When Cliff took her back to Quarterdeck Club, she was no closer to making a decision.

She tried to make up her mind. Should she marry this man or not?

The lone voice of reason came from her father's letters. "Make no compromise with reality!" he implored, repeating what he had said in Germany.

But there was another voice that also whispered to Sabine. It said, *Dance, Sabine! Dance! Don't think so much about it. Take it easy—you deserve this.*

Wasn't Cliff's marriage proposal an invitation to dance?

Meanwhile, as she floundered in indecision, she spent many happy days with Cliff. Little by little, she grew used to his family. And yet, Sabine found their conversations superficial, lightly skipping over reality like the breezes from Biscayne Bay.

"Enchanting! You look spectacular, once again." Sabine grew accustomed to their never-changing compliments.

"The food is simply wonderful," she would parry in the usual "friendliness competition." Whoever had the most flowery speech won. In contrast, if she barely touched on a serious topic, they punished her with disapproving looks.

Always a quick learner, Sabine adapted to this new, shallow lifestyle. Whenever she was unsure of proper protocol, she would smile brightly. Often that was enough to charm whomever she was with. Increasingly, she and Cliff went out with his parents. Cliff's mother soon established a ritual. Before they left, Mrs. Ball would place an expensive mink stole around Sabine's neck. It was rather silly to wear fur in Florida–even in the winter. Sabine knew Mrs. Ball did this to make her more acceptable to society.

Sabine grew accustomed to the round of clubs and restaurants. As the Ball's chauffeur held the door for her, she slipped out of the limousine, feeling somehow important. Even with her inexpensive clothes, which she bought on sale, society mavens adored her. She was a foreign beauty. Cliff noticed the admiring glances and swelled with pride.

Why should Sabine be ashamed of this way of life? Was it bad just because everything was splendid and easy? Increasingly, she listened to the inner voice whispering, *Dance through life, Sabine! Dance!*

And so, pushing down her misgivings, Sabine made her decision. She would marry Clifford Ball.

They celebrated their wedding on an afternoon in March. It was a small, intimate affair, in the Ball's garden, near to the marina. They hired a band from the La Gorce Country Club to play while their guests milled about with their drinks.

About fifty guests attended, mostly close relatives, friends, and significant business associates. Sabine tried to shake off her sadness that only a handful were there for her. No one from Germany was able to make the trip—not even her parents or her brother. Not even Janine had been able to come.

However, no one noticed that the bride's most important people were missing. With a six-course dinner and very expensive champagne, "the most expensive in America," emphasized Mrs. Ball, who thought about the bride's family?

Only Sabine felt the sharp pang. Even when her eyes filled with tears, they failed to understand. "Just look how moved she is!"

As everyone in Germany still struggled to recover from the war, there was no way her parents could afford the expensive trip. But they wouldn't have felt at home in these surroundings, anyway. They were from a different world.

In her heart of hearts, Sabine knew money shouldn't have been an issue. Cliff could have easily paid for her parents' trip out of his pocket change. But something stopped her from asking. In the weeks leading up to the wedding, she kept expecting Cliff or his parents to realize how much she wanted her family at the wedding. Surely, someone would think of them!

No one did.

During the reception, Sabine plucked up her courage and called home. "It's the most wonderful day of my life," she breathed into the white telephone as tears streamed down her face.

On the other end of the line, her father said, "We're thinking of you the whole day. We wish you all the best!"

Though they didn't talk long, the transatlantic call reminded

Sabine how much she missed her family. *Oh, how I wish they could have been here for my wedding day!*

However, as the evening wore on, she was able to forget her sadness. She reveled in every part of the celebration, as every bride should. She wasn't Sabine Koritke anymore. She rolled the words silently over her tongue: *I am Mrs. Sabine Ball!* She was at the very top, just as she had dreamed when gazing up at the skyscrapers of Manhattan. She had reached the goal she had dreamed about for so long.

14

See How the Flowers of the Field Grow

Even the honeymoon was a dream come true–a trip to Europe on the *Queen Elizabeth*. Sabine loved the ship–a luxury ocean liner with ballrooms, and smart state rooms. She loved gliding down the grand staircase on Cliff's arm, and mingling with other guests in tuxedos and gowns. It was vastly different from ships she had previously sailed.

But not everything was wonderful. For one thing, she found her marriage wasn't based on passion. Sabine waited for Cliff to open up, to bring her close. He never did. Instead, he remained withdrawn. Something was missing.

And for another, they weren't alone on their honeymoon! Cliff's parents insisted on coming halfway around the world with them. Sabine wasn't able to tell them no, and Cliff never tried.

However, the Koritke family training took over. She had to be a faithful wife, serving her husband. To act against him or his family was unthinkable.

After arriving in port, they traveled by train to Paris, Barcelona, Rome, and Venice, staying only in the very best hotels. Several weeks into their trip, they arrived in Düsseldorf, where they were to meet her family.

As their chauffeured car pulled up in front of her parents' home on a quiet street, Sabine found she was holding her breath. *What will they think of each other?* They lived worlds apart, separated by much more than miles.

Father met them at the door and shook Mr. Ball's hand with a slight bow. He ushered them into their modest house, presenting them to Mother, then Hans.

Everything went smoothly, contrary to all of Sabine's fears. She breathed a little easier. It was so nice to see her family again, to feel their embrace. Their visit raced by and before she knew it, it was time to leave.

As the two families said goodbye, Sabine clung to Father, crying on his shoulder. She was being torn in two directions. However, the chauffeur was waiting at the curb.

As they were leaving, Mrs. Ball said, "We'd be very delighted if you would come to visit us."

Sabine knew these words were hollow. How could her family ever afford a trip to America? But Mother replied, "Oh, we just can't wait!" In their short visit, her mother had already picked up the Balls' "social language."

As their chauffeur smoothly pulled their limousine away, Sabine thought how different this visit was from her earlier one. Father had held his tongue this time and refrained from lecturing her. However, she could tell from his facial expressions that he had seen right through her new in-laws.

*****

"Here's to your health, Sabine!" Her Miami neighbors lifted

their cocktails in a toast.

"To your health! It's a privilege to have you in our home," Sabine replied.

The five women sipped their drinks. At the end of every afternoon, the neighbors came for a quick cocktail after their shopping excursion, and before getting dressed for another party.

"Sabine you must tell us about your European cruise. We want to know all the details!" said a blond with a deep tan.

So Sabine hit the high points for them–Paris, Rome, Venice. Sometimes she thought her neighbors were a bit too interested in her personal life. Their questions always started innocuously. Then they'd delve deeper.

"Where exactly is Cliff today?" another woman asked.

Sabine squirmed a little. She didn't know the answer to that question. "Away, increasing our wealth," she replied airily, taking a puff from her cigarette. The women laughed as though she had said something terribly funny.

Sabine took a sip of her martini. *Where is Cliff?* It was a question she asked herself repeatedly in coming weeks. Soon after returning from their "group honeymoon," Cliff began to be absent without explanation. He didn't hold down a job. Despite his education in military academy and college, he never had to work a day in his life. His sole responsibility was to manage the wealth he had been born into.

Little by little, their married life began to find its rhythm. They were expected to attend parties, one after another, nearly every evening. They joined some friend or another to cele- brate— what they were celebrating was unimportant. Sabine soon learned the one thing the soirees held in common–the partygoers consumed an enormous amount of hard liquor.

Each morning, Sabine slept late. When she woke, she would kiss Cliff, who also didn't have a reason to get up. She snuggled against him and thought how incredible it was. Every day was like Sunday. Then she fell back asleep in his arms.

The main difference in her life was the safety she had married into. Cliff would never intentionally hurt her. There was nothing to worry about, least of all money. Surely, her father's warnings had been vastly exaggerated.

The morning after their wedding, Cliff gave her a checkbook and a credit card. He told his new bride, "Don't worry. Spend as much as you like."

Sabine did a lot of shopping. Now that she could buy anything she wanted, she paid particular attention to quality. Unlike her mother-in-law, she didn't buy anything ostentatious, even when it was expensive. Sabine kept her German sense of understatement.

She didn't know how much money her new family had. What amazed Sabine was the unlimited flow.

Cliff and Sabine didn't use a chauffeur like his parents. Cliff drove a Cadillac. Naturally, he always had the newest model, usually before it was officially on the market. Every two years, Sabine was expected to choose a new car. Each time, she picked an Oldsmobile convertible. She found Cadillacs a little too flashy.

Several weeks after the wedding, Sabine decided to make another trip home to Germany. For the first time, Sabine traveled by airplane instead of ship. Cliff wasn't able to join her. But she wanted to see her parents again, as well as an old school friend. Monique now lived in Frankfurt.

Sabine never expected what happened to her in Frankfurt. It would change her life.

*****

It was a glorious spring evening. Sabine and Monique were on their way to a birthday party for Herrn von Stein, a well-known Frankfurt architect.

The young women had spent a good part of the afternoon getting ready. The best of Frankfurt society would be at the party. As they stepped into the elevator, Sabine caught a glance of herself in a large mirror. She smiled, glad she had chosen the black silk cocktail dress.

Their elevator hummed its way toward the penthouse. The lift was fitted with brass and mahogany, and sported illuminated buttons. She thought of how this stylish building contrasted with the blackened rubble after the war. It was amazing how fast Germany was recovering.

Sabine linked arms with Monique as they stepped out of the elevator. A valet led them into a vaulted living room where a hum of conversation rose above strains of Mozart from a string quartet. Guests huddled in little groups while waiters in jackets and bow ties wove in and out with silver platters of canapés and champagne.

The party included artists, intellectuals, and business people—prime movers in Germany's postwar resurrection. Soon, Sabine was entertaining people with tales of life in America. As she mingled through the crowd, wine in hand, Sabine was struck by an unsettling thought. *Are we all part of some masquerade? No*, she insisted to herself. *This is reality. It has to be.* She watched Monique laugh at some guest's comment. Why couldn't she relax like her friend and enjoy this wonderful party? After all, they were guests of the distinguished Herrn von Stein.

Still, she couldn't shake it. There was something artificial about the scene.

In any case, it wasn't like the flashy parties of Miami. People didn't flaunt their wealth here. It was merely presumed. Sabine looked down at her heavy diamond ring and quickly turned the stone to the inside of her hand. *Is Cliff's engagement ring a bit too much? And yet... what if it is?* With her newfound wealth, she could more than keep up with any guest at this party. She had made it to the top, moving among the richest people.

Then a more uncomfortable thought hit her. *Am I becoming just like my mother-in-law?* Sabine immediately pushed that from her mind.

Herrn von Stein was an avid collector of modern art. With a little encouragement, he began to show off his finest pieces, guiding the guests from painting to painting, each under its own subtle spotlight.

"And here is my favorite Picasso," he said.

Sabine moved in for a closer look. A shiver ran down her back. Everything about this painting was cold—from the blue in the background to the red of the woman's scanty dress. The colors struck Sabine as forceful, even rude. Hefty brush strokes painted straight lines that met in jagged edges. She decided she didn't like Picasso. This and other paintings Herrn von Stein showed off appeared crass to Sabine. The paintings matched the uncomfortable sense of artificiality at the party.

The air became heavy with tobacco smoke and perfume. Sabine had to get some fresh air. She moved toward an open window and stood there, drinking in the sweet air. The soft light of a spring sun lingered outside.

Now, this is true art! she thought. The last rays of sunshine turned the grass emerald in the courtyard below. She looked down on trees draped with lacy blossoms. In the middle of the courtyard stood a large chestnut tree. Sabine drew a sharp breath. It was striking. Thick branches protruded from its coarse trunk, holding dainty twigs with leaves and blossoms that danced in the evening air.

How many years had this tree stood here? How amazing that it survived the artillery and bombs of war. And how many days would these fragile blossoms last? It was a picture of endurance that was at the same time, fleeting.

Sabine couldn't turn away. This was surely the work of the True Artist.

Then she noticed a tiny woman in the courtyard below, bearing a woven basket. She darted back and forth, collecting laundry from a line that stretched between the tree and a small house. Sabine stood transfixed, watching as she pulled out clothes-peg after clothes-peg, placing her dried clothing in the basket. Sabine took in every detail. The contrast between the woman's faded apron and Sabine's silk cocktail dress couldn't be greater. It was like the difference between good, honest work, and... what?

For an instant, she felt sorry for the woman. The way that she lived, surely that was no life. It must be a miserable struggle for existence. Sabine had everything life could offer. She lived a life filled with sparkling wine and conversation, caviar and Mozart, art by Picasso in a penthouse filled with important people.

Yet, Sabine was uncertain. Her mind tried to reject a truth she didn't want to admit, even to herself. The thought persisted until she could not resist it. *What if I found fulfillment in life as a washerwoman?*

15

My Life is But a Breath

Sabine cringed. How could she think such a thing? *Utter nonsense. No, no, no.* She had reached the very top. She would never give this up.

No! she repeated to herself. *Once and for all, no!* However, deep inside a quiet voice whispered, *Yes, Sabine.*

As the evening light faded, Sabine couldn't turn away from the washerwoman. The woman's rhythmic task of taking down her laundry cast a spell, like an intricate dance.

Sabine submitted to the inner voice. *Fine, then! If I find happiness as a washerwoman, then I want to be a washerwoman.*

She stood at the window several more minutes, flooded with a peace she couldn't explain. Then she felt a gentle tap on her shoulder.

She turned to see her friend, Monique. Sabine was almost surprised to look around and see the elegant party was still going on.

At first, Sabine couldn't speak. Then, in hushed tones she told Monique what had just happened. She told about the secret of the chestnut tree and the woman and how she

85

had heard an inner voice saying she could be happy as a washerwoman. And as soon as she had submitted to this unknown voice, something shifted. It was as if she had made a sacred vow, though she didn't know who she made the promise to.

Monique clasped Sabine's hand. "If you're supposed to be a washerwoman, then that is what you must become!"

Quietly, the two women rejoined the party. They spoke no more about chestnut trees or washerwomen. And yet, Sabine knew she had come to a crossroads. As she stood there in her designer dress, the wife of a millionaire, it seemed impossible. And yet she knew, if life's circumstances made her into a washerwoman, she would be all right.

*****

Sabine leaned against the ample leather cushions in Pan Am's First Class. This trip had allowed her a little longer visit with her family, and she was glad for that. But her mind sped back to that strange premonition as she looked down on the courtyard from Herrn von Stein's window. Would she really become a washerwoman? It was hard to fathom, given her present circumstances.

As the plane dipped for landing in Miami, Sabine caught her first glimpse of the turquoise waters and white beaches lined with palm trees. Although she couldn't explain it, something whispered inside, *I could leave all this, one day.*

Cliff met her at the airport. It took little time to slip back into their shared life. It was good, yet somewhat hollow. Sometimes late at night, she woke up yearning for something more. But she didn't know what she yearned for.

With increasing frequency, she graced the society pages. *The Miami Herald* had prominently featured photos from their wedding. With her beauty and charisma, Sabine proved irresistible to photographers and readers alike. Half the coast now followed details of her life. Sabine Ball rapidly became one of the most recognizable women in Miami.

In the next few years, two wonderful blessings came to Cliff and Sabine: Their names were Cliff, Jr. and Fred, their two sons.

Clifford Howard arrived November 2, 1955. From the moment of his birth, he was a good-natured, undemanding baby. He grew into a happy little boy, the spitting image of his father. And the resemblance was more than physical. Like his father, little Cliff was quiet, thoughtful and content.

On the other hand, from the moment Frederick Walter made his appearance on the fifteenth day of December, 1957, he was his brother's opposite in every way. He was fussy and difficult to console. He was more like Sabine. That was probably why their relationship was often tense throughout the years. Fred grew into a curly-haired little boy who was always active and spontaneous, even volatile.

They hired a nanny to care for the children. The nurse dressed and diapered the babies, fed them, and saw to all their needs. After all, this was what society expected. Later, Sabine would regret that she hadn't cared for her children herself.

The nurse was so efficient that Sabine's life hardly changed when she became a mother. She continued to spend her days shopping, having cocktails with neighbors, and of course, attending the never-ending stream of parties.

Then Father wrote to say Sabine's mother had been diagnosed with cancer. It saddened her. However, she and her mother had never been close. And when Father called in 1961, to say Mother was dying, Sabine decided not to go to her bedside.

She also shoved aside nagging worries about her own life. She treated them like her father's letter of warning from years ago, before she married Cliff. She hid that letter in the bottom of a wardrobe drawer, where it stayed for years. But despite all her efforts, one thought kept forcing its way to the surface: *Am I really happy?*

A disease can spread slowly and quietly, hidden away. A person goes about her normal life, thinking she's healthy until one day—bam! It takes over the body, shocking in its viciousness. The person wonders how she could have been unaware of the monster growing within.

That's the way it is with the poisoning of a marriage.

*****

Sabine sat in a heap on the living room floor, her heart breaking. Tears poured down her face. Her body shook with deep, gut-wrenching sobs.

How long had she been crying? She felt totally spent. She walked across to the stereo and put on her favorite record. Haydn's *Symphony 100 in G Major* filled the empty room. She let the melody wash over her. Sabine felt empty. She had cried so hard and for so long, there was nothing left. She had no tears to cry, no emotions to feel—not love, not fear, not even hate.

An evening breeze floated through the open patio door, carrying the scent of freshly mown grass. Sabine walked out barefoot, onto the lawn.

This must be Tuesday, she thought, digging her toes into the manicured grass. *The gardener comes on Tuesdays.*

She wiped her swollen eyes and wandered out the back gate. Small boats lined the marina, bobbing in the water of Biscayne

Bay. The closer she got to the dock, the fainter Haydn's music became until all she heard was the waves lapping against the piers. She looked far off into the distance. The horizon was an orange stain. The evening's first stars winked in a violet sky. Little by little, the fog in her head began to clear.

She reached their boathouse and rested against a banister. Reaching into her pocket, she unfolded the letter from her father. Today she felt brave enough to re-read it, retrieving it after years in the bottom of her drawer.

Now she smoothed the paper, seeing her father's careful penmanship again.

"Make no compromise with reality," the words leaped from the page. She closed her eyes but couldn't shut out his words. They repeated themselves over and over in her mind.

"Be honest with yourself!" her father's letter implored.

Ten years ago, he had written this letter, warning of the superficial life of the rich. Back then she had closed her mind to his words. Now they haunted her. She carefully folded Father's letter and slipped it back in her pocket. She was ready to be honest. Fresh tears came as she said, "Father, you were right. You were so right."

The last light faded. Today had been a very rough day. This morning, Cliff had packed his bags and left, his face like a stone. He wasn't coming back.

16

Wine is a Mocker and Beer a Brawler

Sabine was reluctant to leave the marina. A warm breeze lifted off the Atlantic and Sabine held herself with folded arms. *How could it have gotten to this point? What's wrong with me, that I can't get along with such a good-natured man as Cliff?*

They had been happy once. Though now, being brutally honest, she knew she had never fallen in love with him. But she had cared for him. They had been good friends.

He never belittled her. Cliff was indeed a satisfied person. He had no pretensions. He wasn't burdened with great ambitions.

She was the one with pretensions. She always wanted more, to get to the top, then go even higher. Cliff wanted to stay where he was. He was a man with neither goal nor vision. At his side, she felt trapped, at a standstill.

"I wanted to be there for you," she whispered into the early night air, "Only to be there for you."

She stared down into the dark water. Cliff was so settled, and she hated that. He didn't wrestle to find fulfillment like she did. He had enough, but she wanted more. But was there anything more? More than what they already had? More than millions of dollars?

In any case, she couldn't drift from day to day as she had done for the past decade. She was sick and tired of going from party to party, from charity ball to opera ball, from one social engagement to the next. And above all, from cocktail to cocktail.

Yes, the cocktails! As far as she was concerned now, they were the devil's concoctions.

She looked down at her hands. She had balled her fists so tightly, her fingers whitened against her tanned skin. *Alcohol. If there was a culprit in our marriage, it was alcohol.*

Drinking had played such a prominent role. At every party, every reception, every social event, in every club… always, always the drinks were there. And always, Cliff embraced them.

It was years before she noticed the cocktails brought more than merriment. Drinking was an accepted part of daily life. And on the rare days when they weren't invited to a party, Cliff drank alone. By noon, his breath would be heavy with alcohol. Sabine didn't think he was driven to drink out of frustration. It was sheer boredom.

Sabine remembered the day she had taken him to task about it. "Cliff, we drink too much," she had said. She tried to make her voice loving, but firm.

"Maybe you're right, dear," was his glib answer, as he refilled his glass.

"Hey, I'm serious about this: You shouldn't drink so much anymore, do you hear?"

Cliff looked surprised. Sabine was serious.

"If you say so…." Grinning, he tipped his glass into a potted plant.

*****

Now as she leaned against the boathouse banister, Sabine remembered that first confrontation. How often she had repeated those same words after that. She had cried and begged, and always his answer was, "I know, dear. I know."

As time went on, his attitude hardened. He grew resistant, unable to feel shame. Over time, Cliff became unwilling to even think of parting with his drinking. And along with that, he gradually lost his wife's respect.

Sabine was an old-fashioned woman. When they married, she wanted to live out her days serving her husband. She had done just that for years. But now, she despised Cliff. She couldn't continue the way they had for the past ten years.

Sabine began to shiver despite the warmth of the evening air. She spoke into the darkness: "You didn't want it different, Cliff. It was you. You messed everything up!"

She was alone on the jetty. No one answered her. Only the waves lapped at the pier.

"Cliff, you're to blame. You alone!" She continued ranting, her fists tightly clenched. Years of anger boiled to the surface.

She remembered how Cliff had tried to hide his addiction. He cleared out the bottles that stood in the living room bar. He took to hiding his alcohol–on the yacht, in the garage, and in the cellar. Again and again, Sabine stumbled upon his hiding places.

For over a year, she kept up her admonishments. Finally, she gave him an ultimatum: "If you drink one more time," she stressed each word, "then I must leave you."

Cliff stared at her, his eyes red and puffy.

"Do you hear me? I will leave you!"

He didn't say a word. But shortly after, his behavior changed drastically. It was as if a demon woke up inside him. For the first time in their marriage, he became very angry. Once in a fit of rage, he even hit her.

As Cliff continued to drink heavily, Sabine phoned his parents. "I will leave Cliff if he doesn't give up drinking," she told her mother-in-law.

To her surprise, Mrs. Ball answered coolly, seemingly unconcerned. Before Sabine hung up, she begged Cliff's parents to come and help.

"But of course, Sabine. We're coming," Mrs. Ball had assured her. What an evening that turned out to be.

Cliff's parents had come immediately. However, as she opened the door to let them in, Sabine heard Cliff call from another room, "Hi Dad! Can I pour you a drink?"

He answered immediately, as if giving his order to a bartender. "Yes, bourbon and water."

For the rest of the evening, they did not once discuss the marriage problems, as Sabine had implored. Instead, they spent the evening drinking. Sabine sat watching them, gritting her teeth. She waited and waited for them to bring up the actual reason for their visit. She was even furious with herself–why couldn't she find the courage to say something?

*****

There was no way to go back and change anything. Sabine lingered by the marina. That evening of non-intervention was the beginning of the end. It sealed the fate of their marriage. They were headed for divorce. Although their marriage limped along for another half a year, it was doomed. And today, Cliff had moved out.

"Now it's over. Everything is over," Sabine said aloud to no one. She drew a ragged breath and squared her shoulders. *It's terrible, but somehow I feel free.*

Father's words from so long ago resonated. "They don't understand true values," he had written about the super rich. "They have no idea what makes a good life."

Sabine turned around and headed back to the house. The record of Haydn had long since stopped playing. She thought about her boys. By now, their nanny would have them in bed.

She found them both fast asleep. She stood gazing down on eight-year-old Clifford and five-year-old Frederick. *They're the best part of my life!* A deep love warmed her and she touched Frederick's curls, still damp from his bath. She looked around the room, taking in the shelves and shelves of the latest toys, and the walk-in closet filled with children's clothes from top designers. She saw it all with new eyes. *We've given them far too much. It's over the top!* And then the realization: *The only thing we haven't given them is values.* Instead, Clifford and Frederick were growing up in a golden cage.

She remembered the ape on the veranda during that party, so long ago. Her next thought came as a shock. *I've also been living in a gilded cage!*

17

I Am With You and Will Watch Over You

She had to take her children and get away from here. They had to escape, not only from the villa, but also from Miami. But where would they go? For years now she thought she had everything. Now she realized she had very little.

Aunt Mary! The thought of her mother's warm, spirited friend brought relief. They hadn't had much contact over the past few years, but she knew Aunt Mary would welcome them. She had left New York some years before and moved to the West Coast. "The most beautiful place in America," was how Aunt Mary described Santa Barbara, California.

Sabine's divorce marked a significant social and financial step downward. When she left Miami, she packed everything in her Oldsmobile. Clothing, dishes, pots and pans, and jewelry. It took her days to drive it all, up Florida's long finger, then across the continent. When she arrived in California, Cliff sent the boys on a plane to join her.

During the divorce proceedings, Cliff had sneered, "You

came with nothing and you'll leave with nothing,"

She remembered that strange premonition in Frankfurt, when she looked down on the chestnut tree in the courtyard. She wasn't worried about being poor, like that washerwoman. But it didn't come to that, anyway. When all was finalized, Sabine left with twenty-eight thousand dollars in her pocket. Besides that, Cliff was ordered to pay seven hundred dollars a month, half for the boys, and half for Sabine. It would be enough to find a small house of her own—enough to begin a new life.

Aunt Mary welcomed Sabine and the boys to Santa Barbara with open arms.

For Sabine and the boys, Santa Barbara was truly a wonderful city, a safe haven of sorts. The location alone was like a dream. Less than one hundred miles north of Los Angeles, it curved along a magnificent bay on the Pacific Ocean. A different kind of palm tree, Egyptian royal palms rustled over streets and beaches. Endless ocean surrounded the city, and mountains plunged to the sea. Spanish-style homes of thick white stucco with red-tiled roofs nestled in the city's many hills. And almost every house featured a breathtaking view of the Pacific.

As Sabine and the boys settled into an apartment, she found the climate less humid than Florida. The air was refreshing, yet never too cool. Delightful. "The most beautiful place in America," as Aunt Mary had said.

Their new life was a big adjustment. Life without a nanny was definitely more stressful. But Sabine wanted to take care of her sons. *They are my top priority*, she reminded herself. However, she found it very hard to be a single mother.

Cliff and Fred felt like outsiders in their new school. And

Fred turned out to be anything but a model student. He struggled with the very act of reading. Although Sabine tried to tutor him, their sessions often collapsed in frustration. Sabine simply had no patience.

One day, it was suddenly too much. She had asked Fred to read a sentence out loud. He stuttered along in tears. "Don't you understand anything at all!?" she yelled before thinking.

Eventually, she hired a teacher for him. He tutored Fred for a couple hours a week, and to Sabine's surprise, got along terrifically. In due course, Fred began to make progress with his reading.

Why couldn't I get along with Fred? Sabine asked herself.

Christmas of 1963 drew near—the first Christmas without Cliff. Sabine bought candles, placing them on tables and cabinets like her mother had always done. As the December days shortened, a mountain of packages arrived from Florida.

The mailman staggered under a pile of gifts for Clifford and Frederick. On Christmas morning, toy after toy tumbled from its wrapping. They were all expensive—typical of the Balls. Sabine was appalled. The boys' father and his parents had sent an invasion of toys to fill their apartment to overflowing. It was enough for an entire orphanage.

Now, there's an idea, thought Sabine.

She tried to calm the boys' greed. "How about choosing every other gift? We'll rewrap them and take them to children who didn't get any presents."

Cliff and Fred, who couldn't even see over their mountain of packages, nodded eagerly. They were generous children.

"I'll give this one to a poor kid, too!" Cliff announced as he unwrapped a model car–a sleek white Cadillac like the one his father drove. However, the longer he looked at the car, the less excited he became about giving it away.

"You may keep it." Sabine smiled, tousling his hair.

Cliff beamed, "I'll give away this one instead!" He pointed to a toy yacht he had unwrapped earlier.

Sabine watched the boys quietly. This was how she wanted to raise her children. They needed to think of others. And she wanted to be a parent like her father, always wise and just.

On the following day, she drove their Oldsmobile filled with treasures to a children's home in Santa Barbara. The children were waiting in a semi-circle. Fred and Cliff walked in with their arms full of toys and the children's eyes lit up.

"This is like my daddy's yacht," said Cliff as he handed the model to a small black boy.

"It's much bigger in real life!" he added, "But I like his Cadillac better."

The boy accepted the boat and looked at it, bewildered.

"Yes, you can keep it," Cliff said, and went on to the next child.

Warmth rushed into Sabine. What a powerful experience, watching her sons give to others! Then, out of nowhere, a sadness stabbed her heart. *What did I do wrong? Why do my sons have to spend Christmas without their father? Did we really have to get divorced?*

She tried to push aside the accusing thoughts.

They said their goodbyes at the children's home and got into their car. As Sabine drove up the canyon toward their home, she argued with herself. *No. There was no way I could've avoided divorce.* She always did her duties as a wife. She organized their household staff to a point of perfection. She saw that meals were on the table at the proper time. She made sure the children arrived at school, well-dressed and punctually.

Dependable and timely, that was how she'd been. She had been the perfect wife.

But something nagged at her conscience. What she thought of as success was exactly what upset Cliff. His weaknesses were glaring when seen alongside her strengths. The more his addiction grew, the stronger Sabine appeared. Her every word and gesture said, "Don't you see? This is how you're supposed to live." Or perhaps, "See what a good wife I am and what a weakling you are?"

She hoped he would pull himself together. Maybe he would take her example and be spurred on to fight—fight against the alcohol, fight for his reputation, fight for her.

However, the opposite happened. The more she pressured him, the weaker he became. With every passing day, she lost more respect until she began to despise him. And she let him feel her scorn.

Now as she pulled up the hill toward her apartment, she realized she had driven him deeper into abyss.

You're to blame, Sabine. You're to blame.

She unlocked the front door and walked into the house. *No! Cliff is to blame. Cliff alone. That miserable drunk!*

She sank into a wing back chair and remembered what her father said when she told him about the divorce: "What did you do wrong in this marriage?"

That was Father's first reaction. He hadn't sympathized with her. He hadn't talked about Cliff. He didn't blame his drinking. He didn't even condemn the super rich, whom he claimed had no true values. No. The first thing he'd asked was what *Sabine* had done wrong.

Father had such an irritating way of speaking the truth. Until this moment, she hadn't been willing to consider his words.

Her friends in Miami had agreed with her. Cliff was to blame. She repeated their assurances over and over to herself. Still, deep down Sabine knew she wasn't being truthful.

18

They are Disheartened, Troubled
Like the Restless Sea

O ne evening at a parent-teacher conference, Sabine
made her first friend in Santa Barbara, Chris
Brainard. The two women clicked.

Right away, Chris invited Sabine over for a visit. Sabine
thought Chris' home was richly decorated and tasteful. But
what she liked most was its openness. Chris regularly hosted
an eclectic group of people.

The atmosphere was very different from the cocktail parties
of Miami. Chris had get-togethers that were less artificial—more honest. Sabine felt comfortable immediately. And
the friends Chris invited didn't boast about their clothes or
material possessions. Instead, they talked about psychology,
culture, theater, and the arts. Sabine felt she had entered a
new, inspiring world.

Chris was the one who introduced Sabine to Marc.

He was an engineer in his forties. Marc was genial, and he
always wore leather boots. He wasn't particularly handsome,
and he drove a modest car. However, his very lack of

pretension drew Sabine. He was confident, and had an unusually deep voice.

Soon the scent of carnations made Sabine think of Marc because he brought her a bouquet each time they met. She had found a gentleman friend, a safe man to help her step into the dating world again. When she left her children with a sitter and stepped out on his arm, she was escaping her past, especially her guilt over the divorce.

She didn't fall in love with Marc, but she didn't miss physical intimacy anyway. Sabine yearned for security, love, and even a sense of duty. She wanted to be needed, to be there for someone, and to care for him. And Marc, so it seemed, needed her care.

Her divorce left her feeling empty and dried out. She thought she'd never find the perfect man, anyway. So why not date Marc?

Her life was spiraling aimlessly, without direction or goals. She was a leaf, blown by the wind. She felt numb inside, neither happy nor sad, good nor bad. Was this the secret to a contented life? Not to feel anything?

One thing did become clear as time passed. She didn't love Marc. When she broke off their relationship, he was heartbroken. But she couldn't commit herself to him.

The next time Chris invited her over, she poured Sabine a steaming cup of coffee, then curled into her Duncan Phyfe armchair. "So, no more with Marc?"

"No. It's over." As she said that, Sabine felt relieved. "Men make life so complicated," she continued. "I'm fine without one. Maybe I should stay that way."

"Come now, Sabine. Don't say things you don't mean." Chris winked and placed her empty cup on the end table. "Besides, I haven't introduced you to Hans yet."

Sabine didn't reply, so Chris hurried on. "You absolutely have to meet him. He's a really great guy. And he's *German*."

She said that as if being German would make Sabine fall for him, head over heels.

"Spare yourself the matchmaking," Sabine said. "I'm serious. I'm through with men."

"But he's German! I'll send him over to your place some-time."

"Fine. Whatever. But don't get your hopes up."

The days became longer and warmer as spring worked its magic over Santa Barbara. One afternoon, Sabine sat in her kitchen with Fred and Cliff, coloring Easter eggs. Warm air wafted in through the window, carrying the song of a goldfinch, and from somewhere further away, the buzz of a lawnmower. Sabine glanced out the window and saw a small black Triumph whiz down the street and sharply brake, screeching to a halt in front of her apartment building. The car door slammed. She hurried to get a closer look, but the driver disappeared by the time she reached the window.

A knock came at the door.

Flinging aside her apron, Sabine called, "Hello! Who's there?"

"This is Hans," came the startling reply.

Sabine opened the door and saw a blond giant of a man. *Wow!* she thought.

Hans didn't say hello. He stood there, raking his eyes over her from head to toe. After a long minute, he said in German, "This is not how I imagined you."

Without missing a beat, Sabine replied, "That's perfectly clear, Mister. And if you think I'm that kind of woman, you

103

can get lost this very minute!" She surprised herself. She had never greeted anyone like that before.

Hans stood there looking dumbfounded and chastened.

"Excuse me. I... er... I'm Hans. I didn't mean to be rude."

"You may come in," Sabine said, relenting.

Hans followed her into the kitchen, taking a seat in the carved oak chair with a high backrest. Sabine had nicknamed the bulky piece "the confessional."

It turned out to be prophetic. This was the first of many visits, where Hans would drop by and take his seat in the confessional, each time telling her a new story of his adventures.

Today, he talked and she listened while continuing to dye eggs with her boys. Soon he had Sabine and her sons laughing.

After a few weeks, Sabine realized Hans was a real Casanova—a textbook example if there ever was one. He was a lovable nut who didn't even understand himself. But he drew women like flowers draw bees. He darted from one relationship to the next, leaving each girl more wilted, unhappier than the one before her. It wasn't long until Hans had left a long trail of deeply disappointed women behind him.

At the same time, Sabine had rarely met anyone as open and honest as Hans. She listened to him, tried to understand him, and just let him talk. He came again and again, taking refuge from his women and from himself in Sabine's confessional.

*****

Sabine knew she and the boys needed a proper home. After searching for nearly a year, she and her realtor drove up one of Santa Barbara's hills. They came to a stop in a cul-de-sac, in front of a white Spanish colonial. The moment she laid eyes on it, Sabine knew this was the house for her. It was somewhat grand, yet homey. Sitting high on the hill with separate balconies on all sides, the house offered a magnificent view of the Pacific Ocean.

When she walked around to the backyard, Sabine gasped in delight. A large, secluded garden was hidden behind a ivy-covered stone fence. In the center of the yard, a fountain sprayed clear water as sunlight created bits of rainbows. Sabine stood there, taking it all in. It couldn't have been more perfect.

They went inside, from room to room. The first floor was remodeled as a separate apartment. She could rent that out, which would help with the mortgage. That still left three bedrooms upstairs for her, Cliff, and Fred.

She signed the papers and they soon moved in.

On the first morning, Sabine walked onto the balcony that opened off her bedroom. She wrapped her robe more tightly and stood watching as the city gradually woke from its slumber. At the city's edge, white waves crashed in from the blue Pacific. She drew a deep breath of the salty air.

"It's a dream!" she whispered to herself, enraptured. What's more, it was her dream. She was living her own dream.

The house cost thirty-four thousand dollars—a handsome price in 1964. However, it was worth every penny to have a home she loved, where she could raise her children.

It was easy finding the first renter, Tom—an Englishman studying at the university. And even better, her boys soon warmed to him. They followed him around, vying for his attention. He also helped maintain the large back yard. In return, Sabine invited him to share supper with them.

Often, Tom brought friends from the university to her table. Sabine welcomed them since she found the life of a single mother was often lonely. However, she didn't want to be taken advantage of. So she charged each one a dollar. Tom's friends considered it a good bargain for a home-cooked meal.

It felt good to laugh and talk with the young people. They loved her stories of Germany and the war, and her tales of high society in Miami. She told how she had walked away from it all, and even about the strange story of the chestnut tree and the washerwoman in the courtyard. For their part, the students opened Sabine's eyes to new ideas and viewpoints.

Eventually, even her blond giant of a friend, Hans joined them for supper every day. He happily paid his dollar, just like the students.

Hans also introduced Sabine to interesting people. They were certainly different than the Miami socialites. There was Marlen, a naturalized American from Syria, and Arvid, a computer specialist. Her new friends made for an eclectic group—newspaper publishers, psychologists, and engineers, to name a few. And like Tom's university friends, they exposed her to new ways of looking at things.

Many times, she drank tea and argued philosophical questions late into the night. Hans, who worked in construction, was bored with these discussions. But Sabine was drawn in.

She began to question herself. *Who am I really? Am I Sabine Koritke? Sabine Ball? Or just plain Sabine?*

For answers, she turned to one of her new friends, a middle-aged woman named Judy Brown, who was married to a psychologist. He worked under the renowned Dr. Fritz Perls, famous for his Gestalt therapy. His ideas about how mind, body, and emotions were unified were growing in popularity. People called him "the new Sigmund Freud." He now offered workshops at the Esalen Institute in Big Sur, further north on the California coast. Multitudes flocked to his workshops.

"Sabine, you have to go to Big Sur," Judy said again and again.

All of Sabine's friends agreed. And so the idea of traveling to the Esalen Institute grew for Sabine. Hans was the only one who didn't jump on this bandwagon. He couldn't imagine anything fascinating about a "shrink."

Sabine's opportunity came the next summer, when Cliff and Fred were visiting their father in Miami. It would challenge Sabine in strange, unexpected ways.

19

Seek and You Will Find

S everal weeks later, Sabine made the drive to Big Sur. She left a day early so she could get used to the new surroundings before Perls' workshop.

As she drove, her mind kept sliding to the issue of nude bathing. She had learned the doctor's courses were known for their liberalness. Among other things, people bathed naked at the Esalen Institute. As Sabine carefully steered her Oldsmobile around each hairpin curve on Pacific Coast Highway One, she asked herself, *Could I dare do such a thing?*

Earlier that day, she was resolute. She would have no part in it! She would never be naked publicly–especially in front of a strange man. And yet now, as she drew closer and closer to Big Sur, her resolve was crumbling.

Something about nude bathing appealed to Sabine. Just thinking about it made her stomach tingle. A pleasurable warmth spread through her entire body.

She shook these ideas from her head. *I won't do it and that's final!*

And yet, how would she handle *not* taking part? Wouldn't it be awkward if everyone else was doing it? Besides, what if it's a pivotal experience for the course, and she missed out?

The Oldsmobile tires squealed around another severe turn and Sabine tapped her brakes. *On the other hand, isn't public nakedness immoral?* For an instant her father's face flashed before her. She forced his image away, focusing on the twisting road.

The view along the coast was breathtaking. Tall cliffs hemmed the road to her right, while the left side plunged to rocks and misty surf, far below. She was taking her time, and not just because this was called "the most scenic drive in the world." It took all her concentration to hug the dangerous curves.

Each turn revealed another fantastic vista. So Sabine decided to pull over at one of the lookouts. She got out of her convertible and stood at the guardrail, breathing in the ethereal beauty. The deep blue ocean stretched as far as she could see. Although the sun burned down, a misty breeze freshened her. The wind blew through her hair—dark brown with silver strands that had appeared this year.

A longing surprised Sabine, swelling from deep within. "I want to be free. Free!" she cried aloud, above the crashing waves.

Just then she noticed a pelican sitting on a boulder jutting from the sea. As she watched, the ungainly bird swept into the sky, impossibly graceful as air currents carried it along. It glided over the waves then settled on another rock.

Sabine spread out her arms and closed her eyes. What if she could be that free, to simply be carried along by the winds of fate? *Only he who jumps learns to fly*, she thought before climbing back into her car.

When she arrived at the Esalen Institute, Sabine was delighted with what she found. If Santa Barbara was a southern Californian paradise, then surely the northern paradise began in Big Sur. Situated at the edge of a national park and poised above a rugged beach, the Esalen Institute was clothed with a dense redwood forest. A stream from higher in the Santa Lucia Mountains cascaded through the property.

As she walked about Esalen Institute, Sabine felt herself relaxing. She poked about the grounds, pausing on a stone terrace above the ocean. Although the air was markedly cooler than in Santa Barbara, the terrace was snug. A windbreak provided shelter from the brisk sea air, and the sun warmed the terrace stones and wooden benches.

Climbing down the stairs leading to the shore, Sabine saw the first of several hot baths. Although she had tried to prepare herself, the sight of a starkly naked young couple in a pool shocked her. They were talking excitedly, paying little attention to Sabine. They seemed unaware of their nakedness. In fact, it was as if they were sitting in a street café, sharing a slice of cake.

Sabine looked away quickly, but the image of the couple burned in her mind. She scurried in the opposite direction, but encountered even more hot tubs.

"Just don't make eye contact, Sabine," she whispered to herself, trying to act as if it were the most natural thing in the world to see pools and cedar tubs filled with folks as naked as the day they were born.

I've got to get away from here!

However, the idea of joining the nude bathing titillated her. She felt the warm tingle again.

Well, there's no time like the present! And, pushing aside all doubts, she peeled off her clothes. She hunched her body a little, darting her eyes back and forth to see if anyone was watching. No one gave her a second glance. A wiry Japanese man was sitting in the nearest tub.

He looks like he's from far away. Maybe I'll be more comfortable being naked with him. A soft breeze stole onto the terrace, sending goose bumps across her body. She wasn't used to being wrapped only in ocean air. Hastily, she slipped into the hot, bubbling salt water.

20

Watch Out for False Prophets

Once in the tub, Sabine's heart raced. *What am I doing?* a voice in her mind asked, over and over. However as the warmth spread through her, she surrendered, and the voice grew still.

This is exquisite! she thought, suddenly flooded with peace and happiness. She laid her head back, watching the wind drive wispy clouds across the sky. She turned to drink in the sight of the ocean and spotted another pelican. She tracked it as the bird dived down, into the ocean.

Sabine stayed in the tub a good hour, feeling that all was right with the world. At last, she climbed out of the tub and leisurely dried herself off. She was no longer ashamed of her nakedness. She felt as free as the pelican she had seen diving into the ocean.

On Monday morning, she entered the dining hall for breakfast and spotted the young couple she had seen in the pool. Before she could help it, a faint smirk rose to her lips. She shook off the image of their naked bodies and sat down at another table.

Suddenly the room grew quiet. A man entered and all eyes were immediately drawn to him. Clothed in a long robe and sporting a flowing white beard, he looked almost like a wizard. *Or an Old Testament prophet,* thought Sabine, though by this time she hadn't read the Bible in many years. *This must be the great Dr. Fritz Perls.*

The hush continued until he sat down.

Already, he had deeply impressed Sabine. Later that day, their group gathered, sitting at tables in a makeshift classroom.

Fritz Perls made his entrance, walking back and forth to graciously greet newcomers. When he stood across from Sabine, looking intensely into her eyes, she was awestruck. Immediately, she felt under his power, drawn in by his charisma. She imagined he could see deep inside her. She'd never met someone who possessed so much authority, such mysterious power. As he gazed into her eyes, somehow he communicated without speaking, promising to lead her to truth and freedom.

She believed him.

When he took his place at the front of the classroom, he paced back and forth while speaking. Then he motioned to a woman at one of the tables. "Come up here and share your story," he said with a soft German accent.

Obediently, the woman walked to the front. She timidly began to share childhood experiences about her mother. "She always screamed at me," she said, barely audible.

Dr. Perls leaned toward her and asked gently, "How did she scream at you?"

"Very loudly." She swallowed, as if the memory was waking after a long time. "And her eyes were so angry when she looked at me."

113

"How did she look at you? Show me!"

When the woman hesitated, Dr. Perls placed a chair in front. "This is now your mother's chair. Sit, please."

The woman complied.

His voice rose and he said, "You are now your mother, okay? Show me how she looks at you."

The woman hesitated, looking at the group.

"Show us all," Perls demanded, his sharp eyes fixed on her.

Little by little, the woman worked into the role of her mother.

Much louder, he said, "Show us how it really was. Show us how loud she was!"

Amid the doctor's shouts, urging her on, the woman worked her way into the role. Eventually, she was screaming at the top of her lungs.

With a swing of his arm, Dr. Perls cut her off. Then, he abruptly changed tone again. He almost whispered. "Now, play yourself. Show us how you felt as a little girl." He placed a second chair across from the "mother's chair."

The young woman looked at him questioningly. Her face was red from screaming. She got up and sat on the other chair.

"Your mother screams at you," he insisted, heavy brows bunching above his penetrating eyes. "How do you feel now? Show us!"

The woman easily slipped into the role of a little girl, the child she had once been. Breaking into tears, she bawled, sinking down into herself.

Sabine was entranced, caught up in the drama. "My good-ness!" she repeated again and again, tears running down her cheeks. She wasn't alone. Nearly everyone was crying by now.

Judy Brown had often told Sabine about "psycho-dramatic

intergroup development." Now she was seeing it before her eyes. *What courage the participants have, going up there and literally coming out of themselves!*

At the same time she thought, *I'll never go up there and perform anything.* And what role would she play, anyway? The conversations with Cliff? How she discovered the bottles of schnapps in the garage? How she had taken him to task for it?

She was much too shy to venture to the front of the class. Bathing nude was one thing, but uncovering her soul? She could never do that.

By Wednesday, halfway through the course, their group had grown quite comfortable with one another. That evening, Sabine was sitting at the bar in the institute's restaurant, talking with another woman from the workshop.

Fritz Perls came in. His entrance no longer left everyone in complete silence. By now, they had grown accustomed to his presence and the aura surrounding him.

He moved about the room, stopping to chat here and there. Then his eyes lit on Sabine, and he headed for the bar. She felt her hands grow clammy.

"Sabine, how are you?" Dr. Perls gazed at her.

"Good, thank you," she replied. Indeed, that was true. She felt better than she'd felt in a long time.

Placing his right arm around her shoulders, Fritz Perls kept looking into her eyes and asked, "Are you really free, Sabine?"

"Yes, I am."

The teacher then draped his left arm around the other woman's shoulders and asked her the same thing. She was a veteran of many courses. She calmly nodded, yes.

He stood there with his arms around the two, then commanded,"Sabine, kiss this woman!"

Sabine quickly pecked her on the cheek.

"No, Sabine. On her mouth." he ordered.

She paused and looked at the woman. Sabine leaned across and kissed her on the lips, immediately pulling away.

Perls' arm still lay heavily on her shoulder. He shook his head. "Kiss her passionately."

Close to tears, Sabine cried out, "I can't do that."

The master dropped his arms, took a step back, and resumed his gentle tone. "As long as you can't do that, you still aren't free."

He turned around and left.

21

Guard Your Heart

Sabine was crushed. She felt as if she had just failed an important exam–as if he had emblazoned a big red "F" on her test paper. She was imprisoned in herself, obviously a hopeless case. She had disappointed this man, whom she had grown to idolize in only three days. Why couldn't she do what he had asked? What blockades were still in her?

"As long as you feel comfortable, everything is allowed," Perls had said.

How can I be so... conservative? The last word hung in her mind like a dirty word. *Conservative.* No. Truly, she wanted to do anything he asked.

Her old weakness for strong men crossed her mind, that feeling of powerlessness against them. When she faced a man of authority, she became small—very small. Just as she had felt with Adolph Hitler, so many years ago. A powerful man left her ready to obey, to follow, to serve. If Hitler had stood physically before her as Perls had done, who knows what she would have done?

117

However, above everything, Sabine wanted to be free. Free from others, and free from herself. Was the Esalen Institute the right place to find freedom?

*****

Long after she returned to Santa Barbara, Fritz Perls' final advice stuck with her."Play a new game, Sabine!"

As time went on, she began to gain perspective on her fascination with Fritz Perls and his teaching. And she began to hear rumors. His sex life was quite debauched, so it was said. Yet, as is the nature with rumors, no one knew the full facts.

Despite the character questions, his words continued to challenge her.

"You do not have to remain what you always were," he had said.

And maybe she felt such a strong connection because he, too, originally hailed from Germany. She wondered if he had truly found what she so deeply sought: freedom.

"Play a new game," she whispered to herself one afternoon as she recognized the hum of Hans' Triumph driving up and parking in front of her house.

Seconds later, she heard him darting up the steps. As was his habit, he burst into her kitchen without knocking, greeting her with a big hug. This time, however, was different. He wrapped his arms around her and didn't let go.

Sabine felt his strength, the powerful muscles of his upper arms and his chest as they lingered. Hans tipped his head down and looked into her eyes. For the first time, she saw his desire. She silenced her conscience and surrendered to her body.

She tilted her head up toward him. His lips felt like fire as they met hers. They stood wrapped in this position for an eternity before he lifted her up and carried her to the bedroom.

*****

Sabine had always said, "Whoever falls for this man, it's their own fault." She knew a relationship with Hans inevitably led to a broken heart. He was a passionate lover who left a path littered with women behind him. Again and again, he let his emotions run wild, misleading yet another girl. As soon as she fell for him, she become stale goods. To the degree he coveted a woman and passionately loved her, he felt just as cold and unfeeling when he dropped her. He despised himself, but he was a slave to his emotions.

At the same time, he was an honest soul. Sabine couldn't help admiring that. He never lied. He never pretended with anyone. Often, he even warned women before sleeping with them, saying he would end up hurting them. No one listened. It only made him more appealing. With his fabulous looks and charm, he cast a spell no woman could resist.

Sabine knew all this. How often had he come and sat in her confessional, crying his eyes out? During every second they made love, she thought, *I'm doing what I've warned others not to do. This will end horribly. It will hurt so much.*

And yet, on the other side of the coin, Fritz Perls had told her to try new things. "Play a new game, Sabine!"

I'm playing, she heard her body answer. She tried to tell herself she wouldn't give her heart away. *I'll hold onto it tightly,* she promised.

Hans and Sabine fell deeply in love. They couldn't live without each other. Often, before a single word was spoken, they anticipated each other's thoughts. Sabine had never known a love like this. She was happier than she'd ever been in her life.

Sometimes she heard a warning whisper, *It's too good to last.* But she quickly pushed the thought away.

After they'd been together nearly a year, Sabine was still happy. And so, when tiny red flags began to wave in front of her, she refused to pay attention. She tried to brush off her worries. *Everything's fine. Hans loves me. After all, don't all relationships go through rough patches?*

Soon, she could no longer deny it. He was tiring of her. The signs were subtle. He smiled at her less often. He didn't want to spend as much time together. Her suspicions grew until she could no longer deny them. The most painful thing to see was Hans, himself. It was sad to watch the fire die in him.

A terrible fear descended on her. *Hans is going to leave me.* If she were honest with herself, she'd been afraid of this since the beginning. Now, her fear was fanned into a giant flame, consuming her. She knew his track record. And yet, she had fooled herself into believing she would be different.

She'd never forget the day she discovered Hans was in love with another woman.

It was a sunny afternoon. She decided to surprise Hans with a quick visit to his construction site. When she arrived, she slid out of her Oldsmobile convertible and stopped abruptly.

Hans was deep in conversation with a young woman. It was something about the way they were standing so close. The way they looked at each other. The woman tossed her blond, wavy hair and laughed. Even from a distance, Sabine could see how they were flirting. Her blood ran cold.

Then Hans looked up and saw her. Panic swept across his face and Sabine saw everything clearly. Somehow she kept her composure and walked toward them. Hans introduced the gorgeous Leslie. It was only afterward, when Sabine reached the safety of her vehicle and was driving away, that torrents of tears erupted. She had to pull over to the side of the road and cry.

She waited a full week before confronting him–a week in which she agonized over what to say. Would he pretend he still loved her? Or worse yet, would he declare his love for Leslie?

In the end, Hans was mostly silent, unable to deny he had fallen in love with someone else. Sabine's heart shattered and a terrible darkness seeped into her soul.

One afternoon, she paced back and forth in her bedroom, crying. *I will never, ever love again!* Why had she given herself so entirely? Hadn't she promised herself she'd hold onto her heart? Every part of her life had become intertwined with his and now he was ripping it apart.

She stood looking out her window, down onto the backyard. Her eyes fell on the garden arch Hans had built. *Everywhere I look, I remember him!*

A bitter taste lay on her tongue. Her mind accused her. *Our love was only based on passion.* They had lived off passion for a year and now the flame had died away. She had no more tears to shed. Only a dull ache tightened her chest. She threw herself down on her bed and a dreadful certainty swept into her: *You can't base a relationship on passion. You have to have commitment.*

She knew now. Without real love, the only result is pain. Stuffing her face into her pillow, Sabine experienced that pain firsthand. For the first time in her life, she wanted to die.

22

Your Wisdom and Knowledge
Mislead You

After awhile, Sabine dragged herself into the kitchen to start dinner for the boys. They'd be home from school soon. Then another memory hit her. The boys, together with Hans! A lazy summer afternoon at the seashore flashed before her and a fresh burst of tears ran down her face. She stood at the sink, tormented.

Cliff and Fred adored Hans. On that summer day, they'd persuaded him to go swimming in the chilly ocean. Sabine sat on the beach, watching as Hans and her sons romped through the waves. Their laughter had carried back to her on the breeze.

*****

Now she grabbed a dish towel and shoved her face into it, abandoning herself to sobs. If only she could turn the clock back!

Sabine had to admit—not all the memories were happy. She remembered a disastrous trip to Mexico, near the end of their relationship. The trip started well as they rode her convertible with the top down, singing along to music on the radio. Things started to sour when they stopped at a restaurant for supper. Hans spent the evening boldly flirting with their waitress, a voluptuous brunette.

"Stop it, Hans!" Sabine complained. But that made him angry. It also set the tone for the rest of their trip.

To make matters worse, they had a traffic accident in Mexico. This infuriated Hans even more. Her car had to be repaired before it could be driven back to California. Hans left Sabine alone in Mexico, finding another way home.

*****

Standing at the sink, she admitted she'd made excuses for his selfishness. She should have seen their romance was over. But she loved him so much.

Over the next few weeks, she was in so much pain. Sometimes it hurt to breathe. Was this the fruit of her so-called freedom? Fritz Perls had urged her to play a new game. Is this how the game ends? She remembered the refrain she'd learned in Big Sur. "As long as you feel comfortable, everything is allowed." Her relationship with Hans had been delightful, but now her heart was a raw, gaping hole. This couldn't possibly be the way life was meant to be.

Some of her student friends claimed there was no meaning to life. It was one of the new ideas they exposed Sabine to around her dinner table. Were they right?

She got a book by Albert Camus. He was one of the philosophers her friends had urged her to read. She read his book dutifully, but as she turned the pages, she refused to believe it. There must be some meaning to life! She longed for it. She decided she would seek for it until she found it.

Meanwhile, she decided to prove herself the better person.

123

Tossing Camus aside, she found paper and pen and started writing a letter to Hans.

She wrote for hours, until her hand muscles cramped and she could write no further. She told him she loved him, and wished him all the best. She ended her letter by warmly inviting him and Leslie over for dinner. She should have known that would be a recipe for disaster.

The night Hans and Leslie came, they all sat under the arbor he had built for Sabine. It was a warm California evening. They sipped their wine as the sun began its nightly dip into the Pacific. Although she tried to smile, Sabine's heart was breaking. Every time Hans touched Leslie, it was another blow. He rested his hand on Leslie's leg, softly stroking her knee in careless intimacy.

How typical of Hans not to bother concealing his passion. It was as though he had never cared for Sabine at all. She kept her mouth clamped shut. Over and over, she silently berated herself. *I've been such a fool.*

Hans just sat there, studying his drink.

The painful evening finally ended when he and Leslie climbed into his Triumph. Sabine stood watching as his sports car disappeared down the hill. What had she hoped to gain by inviting them? Shame him over what he'd done to her? Or perhaps, warn the fair young Leslie?

She shook her head and went inside. No, Leslie was convinced she had found true love. But she would meet the same fate as the women who came before her.

*****

It wouldn't be long until Sabine's search for meaning took a drastic direction. But first, she continued to languish following her breakup with Hans.

124

My life is over. I'll never be happy again, Sabine told herself as the weeks went by. She tried to put on a brave face for the boys, but the minute they left for school, she collapsed in grief again. Each night she lay awake, soaking her pillow with tears. When she finally slept, she dreamed she was in Hans' protective arms. When she woke, it was to the dull throb of reality–he was gone for good.

She suspected things were not going well for Hans and Leslie, either. Several times she heard someone creeping through her back yard and knew immediately it was Hans. Once, she even heard him sobbing as he sat in the garden arbor. It was tempting to rush out and take him back. But Sabine hardened her heart. She even denied herself a little glance out the window. Hans had betrayed her. She would never trust him again.

Over the coming months she rebuilt her life, but it was slow and painful. She spent more time with her sons. However, even there she was unsatisfied. She had to admit that being a mother wasn't as fulfilling for her as for other women. Her spirit yearned for something more. But what was it?

She took up sewing to fill her empty hours. Soon she started selling her creations at Esalen. She often navigated the picturesque but painstaking drive to Big Sur. It felt so good to reconnect with people there–a mixed bag of artists, actors, and dropouts who stayed at the institute year-round. It appeared they'd found the purpose she longed for.

Sabine looked in a different direction. She began to take her sons with her to a Unitarian congregation. This church taught that God was a single entity, rejecting the idea of Father, Son, and Holy Spirit. As time went on, however, Sabine attended less and less. Although she wouldn't admit it to the boys, even she found their meetings boring.

At the urging of her student friends, Sabine signed up for a few lectures at the university. Their classes on philosophy and eastern religions challenged her. She could hardly wait to discuss what she was learning with the students over supper each night.

They even persuaded her to join in their demonstrations against the Vietnam War.

"Of course I'm against the war," she agreed. She marched for peace, but she wasn't sure what she really believed about it.

On a warm spring evening in 1967, a significant choice came before Sabine. As she stood in her kitchen preparing supper, the inviting odor of garlic and oregano wafted through the kitchen. She was in a good mood. Her friend Donna would be joining them for supper. Sabine was putting a bit more spice into a large pot of spaghetti sauce when the phone rang. She immediately recognized Donna's voice.

"Hey Sabine, I hate to impose. But I just found out some of my friends are in town. Could I bring them along to dinner?"

Sabine didn't hesitate. "Of course! I always cook extra." With the students, she never knew who all would show up. She added a little more basil to the sauce. "Who are you bringing?"

"Old friends from San Francisco. Three lawyers, actually."

"That's good! Especially if we stir up any trouble!" Sabine said, laughing a little.

"One more thing," Donna added. "They're all bachelors."

Sabine frowned. "You know I have absolutely no interest in that anymore." Since her disastrous breakup with Hans, she wanted nothing to do with men.

"Well, never say never. At any rate, we'll be there soon."

A few minutes later, Sabine heard her doorbell chime. Despite her earlier protests, her pulse quickened when she opened the door and saw three handsome lawyers.

23

The Wise Woman Builds Her House

Donna introduced Lawrence, Michael, and Jonathan. She said they worked together at a law firm in San Francisco.

Sabine offered them cold drinks in her living room. Soon they were chatting about how scenic Santa Barbara was, like San Francisco.

Jonathan said, "Ah, San Francisco! The city of happy hippies."

Everyone laughed but Sabine. She asked, "The city of what?"

"Hippies!"

When Sabine still looked puzzled, Donna said, "Haven't you seen hippies yet?"

"They're hard to miss," Jonathan said. "They go around barefoot with long, flowing clothes. And they wear flowers in their hair."

"Oh, the guys with long hair?" Sabine said. "I guess I have seen hippies. I just didn't know what they were called. They have lots of them in Big Sur."

Their conversation shifted to the latest hairstyles. Sabine

found long hair on men less shocking than the "mushroom heads" sported by the new band from Great Britain. She had seen a picture on their album and was distinctly unimpressed. "Those Beatles are tasteless!" Sabine said.

Donna and the new friends from San Francisco laughed.

As they moved to the supper table, Sabine said, "Tell me more about the hippies and their long hair."

"Well, it's not just long hair that makes them hippies," Lawrence answered.

Jonathan jumped in. "It's also the drugs."

"Drugs?" asked Sabine.

"LSD, marijuana, hashish...."

Sabine blinked. "What?" She'd never heard these words before.

Michael explained they were narcotics—mind-altering substances. "Lots of people become addicts. They're dangerous," he said, reaching for another piece of garlic bread.

"But, that's awful!" Sabine put her fork down. "Isn't anyone doing anything to help them?"

Her reaction seemed to surprise the others. "I don't really know," Jonathan said thoughtfully. "I've not heard about anyone."

Michael tried in vain to change the subject. But Sabine wouldn't let it go. She kept steering the conversation back to the hippies and their drug problem. And so, over the course of the evening, the three lawyers told what they knew.

They said it was a youth movement, mainly students. They lived together in communes and smoked hashish. "They want to bring peace on earth," Jonathan said, somewhat sarcastically. He added that in San Francisco, they congregate in Haight-Ashbury—a district close to Golden Gate Park.

"So many get addicted and drop out of school," said Michael.

Lawrence nodded. By the look on his face, he was unimpressed with the hippie movement.

Sabine was shocked. All those young people taking drugs, and no one was doing anything to help them!

For the rest of the evening, as the conversation flow around her like fine wine, Sabine sat silently. She couldn't drive the thought from her mind: *Who helps the hippies?*

Long after her guests left, Sabine lay in bed as questions ran through her mind. Moonlight streamed through her window. She wouldn't be able to sleep tonight. She asked herself, *What is going on out there in the world? Things I know nothing about? People are on the verge of drowning... in drugs! And no one's doing anything about it. It's not only extremely irresponsible—it's dangerous.*

The clock in the hall struck midnight, and Sabine gave up on sleep. Throwing back the covers, she got out of bed and paced about her bedroom. The more she paced, the more agitated she became. *It isn't right! Why isn't anyone doing something?* A great injustice was being done to the youth of America, and no one cared!

Maybe President Johnson should do something, perhaps initiate a program. Or, what about everyday citizens in the community? Surely there were good people who could help troubled youth.

...Good people? She stopped pacing and stood at the window, staring out at shadows in the garden. *Is anyone truly good?*

She thought of people in her life. They were all nice enough. But did anyone live with integrity? Her eyes fell on the arch standing in the moonlight. *Hans, for instance.*

At first she'd only seen his good qualities. Now she knew

how thoughtless and cruel he could be.

Suddenly, she saw a pattern. From her marriage to Cliff, to how enamored she had been of Fritz Perls, to her affair with Hans–Sabine saw the same thing repeating itself. At first she'd be blind to anything but the good in someone. But then another person would fail her, and she'd end up burned.

Was she destined to repeat this pattern, over and over? Would everyone and everything let her down? Maybe the university students were right. Perhaps it was all meaningless. Maybe God didn't exist either.

And, what about me, Sabine Ball? Am I a good person? The question came out of nowhere, taking her breath away. In the dark solitude of her bedroom, she knew the answer. *I'm no better than anybody else. In fact, I'm even worse! I'm always disappointing people in my life.*

She stood there, unable to move. It was very quiet, in the house and outside. But accusations flew up inside her. *I've also left a pathway of wounded people behind me!* She had let down her father, ignoring his advice and marrying into high society. She had rejected her husband, refusing to give him another chance. And she had refused to go to Hans when he cried in agony in her garden. And what about young Cliff and Fred? Was she treating them fairly?

She tore herself from the window, resuming her frantic pacing around the dark room. What was her life? It was nothing but a sham! She caught her shadowy reflection in the dresser mirror. Her hair was wild and her eyes frantic.

"An illusion. My life is nothing more than illusion," she said to the stranger in the mirror. *Am I going crazy?* She noticed the tears streaming down her cheeks. *What am I here for? Will I be buried under the earth after eighty or ninety years and my life have counted for nothing?*

Despair wrapped its tentacles around her, making it hard to breathe. If her life was for nothing, if everything was meaningless, what was the point of living? What was to stop her from ending her life right here and now?

She remembered the prescription bottle in her medicine cabinet. How many pills would it take? In a few short minutes, everything would be over. Would she finally be at peace?

"It would just take a few tablets," she whispered to the ghost in the mirror. She turned away from her image. The rational part of her brain warned, *Come on Sabine, go to sleep. Tomorrow the world will look different. Don't make a fool of yourself because of a few crazy hippies....*

The hippies! There they were again. Abruptly, her mind raced, once again fixating on the hippies. *Who helps them? Who cares for justice? Who takes responsibility?*

A ten thousand volt hit her: *Maybe the hippies need me! Maybe that's my purpose in life."* If no one else was willing, maybe it was her calling to help them.

Suddenly, it was all too much to think about. She climbed back into bed, and within moments was fast asleep. For the rest of the night she dreamed of multitudes of lost young people with flowers in their long hair.

24

Children Sitting in the Marketplaces

Over the next few days, Sabine couldn't stop thinking about the hippies. She thought of their plight constantly—while at the park with her sons, and while running errands. They even invaded her dreams when she was sleeping. She turned it over again and again. What could she do to help them?

An answer came. She must get to know them, to be their friend and see how they live.

In order to get a fresh beginning after breaking up with Hans, she sold her silver convertible, trading it for a new yellow pickup truck. She used it to drive herself to San Francisco.

Her trip had one objective: to meet and learn about hippies. Sabine had only a hazy idea of how she was going to do this. Her plan was to locate the district of Haight-Ashbury. Once she actually found the hippies, she'd follow whatever path opened up.

At least she had a place to spend the night. Her students had introduced her to David, a gay man who lived in San Francisco. David kindly invited her to stay at his home for the

133

night. And since her sons were away, visiting their father in Miami, nothing was holding her back.

Now if she could just find Haight-Ashbury. She maneuvered her truck through San Francisco traffic, navigating one heart-stopping hill after another. Her map gave a general idea where she was going. Once she got close, surely someone could point her in the right direction.

Driving down Dolores Street, Sabine saw two ornate towers–a tall one beside a shorter one. As she drew closer, she saw that they sat atop a magnificent, Spanish-style basilica. A wooden sign on the lawn read, "Mission Dolores." Sabine knew this famous church was near to Haight-Ashbury. Its original name was Mission San Francisco de Asís, named for St. Francis of Assisi. And the city was named after this mission that dated back to the Spaniards.

She pulled over and parked her truck. As she climbed out, she remembered what one of the lawyers said. "Haight-Ashbury is a dangerous place. Don't go alone. If you must go, stay in your vehicle with your doors locked and your windows rolled up."

However, Sabine decided to throw caution to the wind. How could she meet hippies if she drove by in a locked vehicle? She had to get out, walk around, and talk to them.

She stopped an elderly woman on the sidewalk. "Excuse me, ma'am. Could you tell me how to get to Haight-Ashbury, please?"

The woman looked at Sabine. "Are you sure you want to go there?"

Sabine nodded.

"It's behind that hill," she pointed. Then added, "I'm not sure what your business is, dearie, but it's not a safe place."

"Thank you," Sabine said quickly. "I'll be fine."

The woman shook her head and walked on down the street.

Sabine went back to her truck, retrieved a jacket and a small handbag, then re-locked it. "Until tomorrow," she whispered to her new pickup.

After a half hour of steady walking, she came upon Haight Street. Seeing the street sign suddenly made it real. *What on earth am I doing?* Her heart began to pound. Had she been foolish, coming alone as a single woman? *It's not too late to turn around and go home,* a voice in her mind whispered.

No, I can't turn back now! Sabine countered. She kept walking.

Three-story Victorian buildings filled the neighborhood, each in a different stage of disrepair. A defiant mix of stores lined Haight Street, offering garish art, boutiques with embroidered jackets and peasant skirts, shoulder bags, and exotic jewelry, shops with musical instruments and drums, occult bookstores, tea shops, and an establishment with the strangest assortment of pipes Sabine had ever seen. One was a tall water pipe, like something out of *Arabian Nights.* Curious, Sabine went close to the window, cupping her hands around her eyes to see into the darkened store. *What an odd place!*

Sabine stepped over a garbage-strewn gutter. As the afternoon shadows lengthened, people began to fill the street. It reminded her of street festivals back home in Germany. Except here they looked like people from another time in history.

Sabine walked among them, noticing all the young girls had flowers in their hair. Some wore a single bloom, and others wore garlands. Sabine remembered, hippies were also called "flower children."

Their bright clothing flowed freely, and Sabine noticed the girls weren't wearing anything underneath. The young men intrigued Sabine. Their hair hung long and free, and most had beards. Nearly everyone was barefoot.

Sabine passed many clubs, with the sound of guitars and drums and laughter spilling out. Over the stench of alcohol and stale smoke, a sweet, cloying smell wafted through the air–some strange type of tobacco.

She came upon a circle of young people sitting on carpets laid right on the sidewalk. They were humming together, and they looked somewhat transfigured. Sabine was struck by how laid back everyone was.

Across the street, a man was selling clothes, towels, and blankets, piled on a folding table. Three girls were picking through the clothes. Abruptly, one girl–maybe she was sixteen–pulled her dress off over her head. Sabine thought, *At least this one's wearing a bra and panties!*

The girl casually slipped into one of the dresses the man was selling.

Well then! Sabine stood rooted to the ground. People had shown more nakedness at the Esalen Institute. *But this is a city street!* She had entered a culture where people knew no shame.

She remembered her former mother -in-law in Miami's high society. Sabine was definitely in a different world now. It drew her in.

Approaching the ones sitting in the circle, she asked, "How are you all doing?"

"We're wonderful! Sit down. Join us."

When she sat down, the heavy odor of sweat, musk, and patchouli assaulted her. But as she stayed with them on the sidewalk, she found they were eager to share their beliefs. And they did more than answer her questions. They embraced Sabine. Before the circle broke up, they invited her to share a meal with them. She went with them to Dolores Park, where they spread out makings for sandwiches on a picnic table. As they ate, they told Sabine their goals: They wanted peace in the world, they wanted to live a simple life, maintain their community, and have time for one another. Sabine felt a connection.

Dusk gathered in the park, and Sabine sat down on blankets they spread on the grass. She took a bite of her cheese sandwich. Not everything about the hippies was great. The biggest drawback was how dirty they were. She tried not to think about their careless hygiene while making the sandwiches. But ultimately, she wanted exactly what they wanted. A life with meaning. Their open, honest ways also touched her. Their revolutionary spirit, their will to change the world, their boldness to stand up for what they believed–all these things, she admired.

As she watched, she noticed some were buying and selling drugs, right there in the park. That shocked her. Although they talked about peace and love, Sabine realized they were using drugs to escape reality. Several told her they came from wealthy homes. One young man said, "I just had to break out of the golden cage, you know?"

She knew exactly what he meant.

Much later that evening, Sabine met up with her host, David, at the spot they had agreed upon. She followed him in her truck, going to his house—another Victorian three-story. But unlike the shabby ones in the hippie neighborhood, David's house was neatly painted in light blue with white trim.

He introduced Sabine to some of his friends, who were also homosexual. It was an eye-opening experience. She learned David and his friends were part of a large gay community in San Francisco. She liked them immediately. Sensitive, creative, and educated, they were all interesting men. Sabine believed their sexual leaning was unnatural, but that didn't stop her from getting close to them. In fact, she felt safe around them.

Sabine ended up staying a few days with David. She spent her time visiting with the hippies she'd met on her first evening in San Francisco. They invited her to their communal house, where she joined them in preparing and sharing meals.

One day they were eating hearty vegetable soup, sitting on the sagging floor of what must have once been a proud family dining room. Sabine had an idea.

"What you need is a function," she said. She feared that without a job and a sense of fulfilling daily goals, the hippies would fall into despair.

"You're so gifted…" she continued. She had marveled over the handcrafts they made and sold. "If you were given a chance, you could go far!"

No one answered her. But later, as she drove back to Santa Barbara, she thought how they needed a place. Somewhere out of the city. And tools. Maybe if they came to a country place, and worked at something fulfilling, they'd not need the drugs anymore.

25

I Have Raised You Up for This Very Purpose

Before she pulled into her driveway, she'd made up her mind. She'd start looking for a suitable piece of land, up near San Francisco.

Cliff and Fred were still away in Miami and Sabine found her house far too quiet. She decided to close it up and head to Big Sur for the rest of summer.

She fell in love with a charming rental there, a small wooden cottage on the property of a landscape architect named Doug Madson. She loved everything about the cabin and its setting—one of several scattered over Madson's large property. Each cabin boasted a spectacular view of the ocean. In the middle of his land was a meadow, centered with a swimming pool.

The only drawback was Doug himself. It wasn't because he was gay. Sabine was tolerant, like everyone else in Big Sur. But the tight-knit community agreed–they didn't like Doug.

He had devised a scheme of renting his cabins inexpensively to young people. In return they agreed to fix up their place.

However, after renters put a lot of effort into their cottage, Doug would promptly evict them so that he could rent it as a vacation home. It was no wonder he was so unpopular.

However, Sabine often found something to like in unlikable people. From the beginning, she and Doug got along well. She ended up helping decorate his large house, and even shopped, and cooked meals for him. For his part, Doug turned out to be a gifted designer. They had similar tastes. He impressed Sabine with the quality he used. He furnished his redwood rental cottages with Persian rugs, animal skins, and handwoven blankets, creating a welcoming, earthy feel. In the front of the cabins, he planted a rose garden with a whimsically placed antique bathtub set among the flowers.

One summer evening, she was walking through the wildflowers in the meadow at the center of Madson's property. The late day sun caught the blue of lupines, the red of coast paintbrush, and the oranges and yellows of poppies, making them burst to life. What a perfect time for dreaming.

Sabine mused, *If I buy land for the hippies to live on, I want it to be exactly like this.*

But, wait. What was she thinking? Did she believe that she, a lone woman, could start such a place? And would the hippies be willing to leave behind their drugs for a new life?

She stopped still. *Is this the purpose of my life?*

It was a question that grew and grew in Sabine's mind. But it took a dangerous encounter to confirm her direction.

She had found a favorite place to spend leisurely evenings, the Nepenthe Restaurant. It perched eight hundred feet above the Pacific, a gathering place for artists, intellectuals, and to Sabine's delight, hippies.

One evening, she dressed and put on her makeup, looking

forward to another evening at Nepenthe. Under her breath, she sang a tune she learned from the flower children on Haight Street. "Purple haze all around, don't know if I'm comin' up or down...."

She carefully dabbed on a bit of eye shadow, then paused to study herself in the mirror. Sabine approved the way her embroidered blouse and peasant skirt skimmed her body. Although she was the mother of two sons and in her forties, she still looked good. She could still turn many a man's head when she walked into a room.

"I've still got it!" She winked to her reflection, picked up her handbag and headed out the door.

Sabine never expected to be in danger before the night was over. She left her car parked outside the restaurant. After a blazing sunset, an ocean breeze picked up and tiny goose bumps prickled her arms. Heading inside Nepenthe, she slid onto a stool at the bar and ordered a glass of white wine. The beginning of another relaxing evening among the kind of people she liked.

Three stools over sat a burly, dark-haired man. Sabine took his measure. He wore blue jeans and a plaid flannel shirt, with the sleeves rolled up to reveal a massive tattoo snaking down his arm. The man was enormous. His hands were thick and strong, and his fingers looked as if they could hold an iron grip.

He's a little like Hans, thought Sabine. Then, *No, that's not right. No one could compare to Hans.*

After about two minutes, he looked over and smiled at her.

"Hello!" he said in a soft drawl, sounding a little like John Wayne.

Sabine smiled back, but not in the provocative manner she

had fine-tuned over the years. She no longer wanted to play with men's emotions. Not after she'd been burned by Hans. All she wanted was friendly conversation.

Despite her apparent reserve, the man took her smile as an invitation. He scooted over next to her.

"Alone here?"

"No. I'm not alone. There are nothing but nice people all around me!" Sabine smiled cheekily.

The man introduced himself as Daniel, a plumber from Big Sur. From his first sentence Sabine could tell he was a bit drunk. He was a soft-spoken man, and she guessed that the liquor gave him courage.

Within minutes he told her his entire life story. At fifteen, he had run away from his home in Houston, Texas. His father had often beaten him. Daniel's eyes grew sad as he told how his dad had beaten his mother, too.

"I just couldn't take it anymore," he said, "I had to get out of there." He hitchhiked all the way from Texas to California. "I guess I was seeking the freedom of the west," he shrugged.

"And did you find it?"

Daniel laughed out loud, and tipped his glass at her, "No, I got me a job. I lay waterlines and fix stopped up toilets." He gave a hollow laugh. "Damn freedom!" He took a sturdy swig and banged his glass on the counter.

Sabine didn't know if his story was true or not, but she recognized a hurting soul. She told him she, too, was from the East.

"Pretty far east, I take it?" Sabine's accent was always a dead giveaway.

She found herself telling him about growing up in Germany, then of life in Miami, mentioning casually that she was divorced. Daniel was curious about Hitler, and what it was like during the war. He listened intently as Sabine told about Dresden and Dessau, about air raids and phosphorous bombs and Hitler's big lie.

She finished her story by telling of leaving Miami. "I decided to come west for a new beginning."

"Go west, huh?" Daniel grinned, exposing yellow teeth. "Yes. Go west," Sabine said. That was what connected them: beginning a new life in the west.

They passed the evening talking, drinking, and smoking cigarettes in the bar. It was not a particularly sophisticated conversation. Talking to him was just a way to pass an otherwise quiet evening.

After they each paid their bill, Daniel suggested going to a bar nearby. Sabine agreed. She accepted a ride to the bar in his truck, leaving her yellow one parked at the restaurant. The Anyway Bar was only a few streets away.

Once inside the bar, he ordered a German beer. "In honor of Sabine," he said in his Texas accent, grinning at her.

A soft male voice behind her surprised Sabine.

"What a surprise! Hello, Sabine."

Turning, Sabine discovered an old friend from the Fritz Perls course at Esalen. "Why hello," she smiled, accepting a quick hug and peck on the lips.

She couldn't see the look that bore itself into her back. Daniel exploded. His fist shot past her head, connecting with the shoulder of her friend.

"This is my woman!" he bellowed, dragging the man across the bar and outside. Throwing him to the ground, Daniel screamed with rage, all the while pounding him on his face, his chest, all over. Her friend fought back, and a fierce brawl began.

Each man's fighting ability surprised the other. The plumber's strength was matched by his opponent's speed. By now, the bar's patrons were all outside, watching the fight. But no one dared come between the flailing fists.

"Please Daniel, stop!" Sabine cried over and over, to no avail. He was as good as deaf, battling like a wounded bear. Someone called the police and they broke up the fight. After taking down their information, the cops sent them both home and left in their patrol car.

Sabine's friend beat a hasty retreat, leaving Daniel sitting on the curb. A few onlookers offered to drive Sabine home, but instead she sat down on the ground beside Daniel.

"You don't want to ride home with me anymore, do you?" Daniel muttered, his head down.

"No, no. I'll ride with you," Sabine said. The onlookers looked surprised."Ain't you afraid of me at all?"

"No, I'm not," Sabine answered, without the slightest doubt. Something inside said, *Sabine, you need to be there for this man.* She wanted to show she still trusted him. If she left him sitting on the dirty curb, something in him would die. She wanted to reassure him, to literally help him to his feet.

She got up, then reached down for his hand. "Come on, Daniel! We'll drive home together." Daniel looked as if she were offering him a precious gift, treating him with a dignity he didn't deserve. Tears sprang to his eyes and he stood.

Sabine hoped he was sober enough to drive. He steered his truck onto Highway One, along the steep coast.

26

Do Not Worry About Your Life

The road hinted of danger. Far below each perilous curve, waves hurled themselves against the rocks. The moon cast an otherworldly light on the sea.

They drove in silence. Sabine tried to make sense of the craziness of that fight outside the bar. All of a sudden, Daniel veered off Highway One, onto a deserted road leading into the mountains.

Sabine was shocked to see the change in him. It was as if someone had reached into his mind and flipped a switch. Gone was his gratitude for her forgiveness after the fight. Instead, a hardness came over him. She could see it in the way he clenched the steering wheel. And he was taking short, hard breaths.

Her heart began to trip.

Daniel stopped the truck at a lookout next to a precipice. Sabine recognized it as one of many lookout points where tourists stopped in the day to take pictures. At night there was no one in sight.

He cut the motor and an absolute silence filled the vehicle. Moonlight streamed through the truck's dirt-streaked windows, and Sabine could see the madness in his eyes.

"I'm gonna rape you," he said in a voice of steel.

His words cut into Sabine, but at the same instant, her mind saw everything very clearly. She knew exactly how much trouble she was in. At the same time, she felt enveloped by a strange calmness. She hadn't thought of God in years, but a covering of peace and love descended on her.

She thought of trying to escape, but knew she could never outrun him. And she couldn't defend herself against this powerful man.

Daniel gripped the truck's hand brake. His eyes scraped along her body, her soft white neck, then focused on her breasts. He was seconds away from ripping off her dress.

"You know you want it," he said thickly. "You're nothin' but a dirty tramp. I'm gonna rape you!" he said again, his words tearing into her flesh.

And then suddenly, she knew exactly what to do. With a firmness that even surprised her, she looked Daniel in the eye and said quietly, "No. You will not rape me." Placing her hand on his, which was still holding onto the hand brake, she looked him straight in the eyes, forcing him to meet her gaze.

After a minute, Daniel faltered, slowly letting his hand drop from the brake to his side. It was as if a demon was suddenly cast out of him. Sabine sensed his emotions shifting from raging lust to deep shame.

Tears rolled down his cheeks, and he slumped against the seat. He was as good as paralyzed.

"I can't do anything to you," he babbled. "What power do you have over me?"

"Put the key in the ignition and take me home right now,"

Sabine commanded.

Daniel obeyed. They didn't speak again until they reached her little cottage on Doug Madson's property. As she reached for the door to get out of the truck, she turned back to him one last time. Her words surprised her. "I'd like to see you again."

His eyes widened in shock. He hadn't expected this. But Sabine knew in the core of her soul that Daniel needed a friend.

Pursing his lips together, Daniel said softly, "Okay."

Sabine smiled, touched his hand for a fleeting second, and whispered, "Goodbye, Daniel." Before she had a chance to fully shut the door, he had peeled away, the thunder of his truck disappearing into the night. She never saw him again.

She lay in the quietness of her cabin that night, unable to sleep. The questions that plagued her all summer rose again, plus a new one. *Can I prevent others from doing evil?*

Daniel's earlier words repeated in her mind. *What power do you have?* She had faced down the most wicked, evil side of Daniel. And somehow, she had overpowered a much larger man with only her words. She had found a way to break through his madness, to appeal to the part in him that was good.

Then, even in the safety of her bed, a violent shudder ran up her back. "I'm gonna rape you." His words ran over and over in her mind. She had just looked the devil in the eyes, hadn't she? And she had driven him away with a simple word! Wasn't that something like a calling?

Suddenly, an idea dropped into place. *If I prevented Daniel from evil, I can help the hippies.*

It was a week later, and the trauma of the encounter with Daniel was fading. Sabine was working in the rose garden in

147

front of her cottage, lopping off dead blossoms. She looked up to see a man going to the swimming pool in the middle of Madson's meadow. He looked familiar. She'd seen him a few times at the Nepenthe.

It was a hot day, and as she leaned over her rose bushes, she saw him strip off all his clothes and plunge into the pool. When he came up for air, he spotted Sabine and gave a little wave before diving under again.

After taking the course at Esalen, Sabine wasn't as shocked by public nudity. In fact, she found this carefree behavior natural, and rather exciting. She often lay naked in the hot sun on Madson's terrace. Knowing her landlord was gay made her feel safe. She was glad she had lost the inhibitions and feelings of shame she once had.

She kept clipping her roses, but stole looks at the giant of a man, enjoying himself in the water. He had thick black hair that grew down past broad shoulders. His face was covered with a heavy beard. From what she'd heard at the Nepenthe, he was sort of a guru among the hippies in Big Sur–a natural leader.

Leisurely, the man climbed out of the pool, dried himself, and put his clothes back on. He walked over to Sabine.

"Hi, I'm Gus." He smiled at her.

At that moment, a young woman in a flowing white gown entered through the garden gate. She had long brown hair, and Sabine saw immediately that she was pregnant.

"This is my wife, Mary," Gus said with obvious pride, putting his arm around her.

The three sat down in the grass by the rose bushes, spending the rest of the morning talking. Gus and Mary impressed Sabine. They both had remarkable looks. Mary told Sabine that Gus was "a distinguished hunter and fisherman." He was also a good carpenter, and occasionally worked for Doug Madson.

Sabine found Mary enchanting. She was as sweet as she was pretty. Her soft beauty reminded Sabine of princesses in German fairy tales.

She learned Gus and Mary lived in a teepee, like the ones in western movies. Gus had patterned it after the ones made by Native Americans. They had their teepee on the edge of the redwood forest.

Sabine listened, enraptured, as they told of their lifestyle, and about other artists, potters, and painters who called Big Sur home. Their idyllic life captivated her, calling to something in her spirit.

I want to live like that! The words sprang from her heart after Gus and Mary left. *I want to live with the flower children.*

She knew with utter certainty: If the hippies had any chance, they'd have to leave the city. That atmosphere dragged them down into drugs and other dangers. If they lived simply, out in the country close to the earth, they'd find freedom. And as she helped them do that, she would discover true meaning and purpose for her life.

When the summer wound down, Sabine said a sad goodbye to her redwood cottage and went home to Santa Barbara. But something new was around the corner.

Sabine met Cliff and Fred's plane at the small Santa Barbara Airport. They were returning from Florida, bubbling over with excitement. The boys took turns telling all about a yacht trip with their dad on the Atlantic Ocean.

She could hardly believe her eyes when their bulging suitcases came out of the baggage gate. They looked like they were about to pop open! Sabine knew their bags were filled with extravagant gifts from their grandparents.

She helped them lug it all outside to her yellow pickup. As she pulled onto Hollister Avenue, Sabine wondered how she was going to tell them she was selling their lovely home in the hills of Santa Barbara.

27

I Will Bring You Back to This Land

Starting a new life on the land was all Sabine could think of now. Her lawyer guests had planted the first tiny seeds of the idea back in the spring. Now it had grown into a full-fledged dream. Everything, from her trip to San Francisco, finding hippies who needed her help so much, to her dramatic encounter with Daniel, all added up to one thing. She was confident she could turn people from evil acts. Meeting Gus and Mary also inspired her to achieve their simple, happy life.

At first, however, life fell back into its usual pattern. The boys went back to school. Sabine began to cook meals again for the university students. Her dreams were shoved to the back burner.

Then one day in the fall of 1967, she heard about a new hippie oasis. They were flocking to Mendocino, a secluded fishing village about one hundred and fifty miles north of San Francisco. She knew she had to go, to see what was happening. After leaving her sons with a reliable babysitter, she drove her truck from Santa Barbara, nearly five hundred miles north.

When she passed through the redwood forests and pulled into Mendocino, Sabine realized she'd found another treasure along California's Highway One. She was swept away by its rugged beauty. Situated on a headland, with the Pacific on three sides, the landscape was a fantasy. Formations crafted by wind and ocean currents of long ago rose out of the sea. They took the shape of hollowed bridges, cones, and smooth pyramids.

The town featured plank-sided storefronts that looked like the set of a western movie. Flower children had already moved into the small town, some sharing old houses, and some in newly-founded communes.

Sabine noticed that while Mendocino didn't have the classic flair of Big Sur, it was quaint and pleasant. The air was salty and cool, the city was far away, and above all, the prices were low.

As she drove back to Santa Barbara, she wondered, *Should I move to Mendocino? Is it the next chapter in my life?*

It was a difficult decision. After all, not long ago she said she'd spend the rest of her life in Santa Barbara. And her life was safe here, with good friends and a comfortable home.

However, something urged her to reach for her dreams. She craved a challenge that consumed her, that gave her purpose and meaning. She knew she'd always regret it if she passed up this opportunity. How could she live with herself if she refused to make a difference?

So, her mind was made up. Once again, she'd pull up stakes and tackle something new. Sabine spent much of the winter months preparing to move. She talked it over endlessly with friends. All of them encouraged her to follow her dream. They admired her courage, as she jeopardized everything for what looked like a crazy idea. By now, everyone had heard of hippies. Most felt sympathy for the new movement. Yet none of them would have considering leaving everything behind to do what Sabine was doing.

She put her house on the market, and was pleased when it sold quickly at a handsome price. She sold all her jewelry to a former friend from Miami, who also bought a cabinet filled with silver, cutlery, decanters, and bowls. Sabine even sold the engagement ring Cliff had given her.

Now she had nothing left to tie her to her former life. Those luxuries were relics from another world.

Her students helped with the move, loading all the possessions that Sabine had not sold into her truck and two friends' cars.

Sabine was about to drive off with her boys when she gave a final glance back at the house. To her amazement, a man stood on the front steps, clutching a bouquet of white flowers. She hadn't seen Hans in more than a year. Yet there he was, a ghost from her past. One look at his red eyes told her he'd been crying.

Getting out of her vehicle, she walked up the steps to him.

"Sabine, why didn't you wait?" he asked softly.

"Wait? For what?" She brushed past him, unlocked the door and went inside.

"For me! until I was ready" he said, trailing behind her. Sabine moved quickly through the house, looking one more time into each room.

She checked the kitchen. Behind her, Hans whispered, "Could you still love me?"

"It's over, Hans," Sabine said sharply, heading into the next room. "You know that. We'll never be together again."

Fresh tears filled his eyes. She turned away.

"But you belong to me," he hollered, stomping after her like a defiant child.

"It's time to go now, Hans," she said, more gently. He tried to press the flowers into her hand, but she threw them on the kitchen counter.

"Come on." She walked to the front door. "It's time to go."

She could see the devastation in his eyes. Walking out the door, he sank onto the front steps.

Sabine locked the house and walked past him. Before she climbed into her truck, she turned and called out. "Bye, Hans. Live well!"

The last she saw of Hans, he was sitting on what used to be her front steps, sobbing. She had left his flowers behind in the kitchen where they would wither and die.

*****

"Just wait until we get to Mendocino!" Sabine said to Cliff and Fred as they made the long drive. "You're going to love it there!" Her truck ate up the miles, heading north on Highway 101.

She told the boys about the forests of giant, old redwoods, and about the wild sea where they could play among giant rocks.

"And best of all, boys, we're going to live with the hippies!"

She looked over at her sons. They were awfully quiet. "The hippies are extremely dear people," she said.

Cliff was a teenager now, and Fred was eleven. Considering how drastic a change this would be, they had put up surprisingly little opposition. Although truthfully, Sabine hadn't given them a choice. She hadn't asked their opinion. She made the decision and that was final.

And why should she ask them? After all, she was their mother. She made the decisions. It was their duty to follow. Besides, they were kids–they would adjust.

The years in Santa Barbara had flown by. How long would they live in Mendocino? Sabine no longer dared to make a prediction. She thought she and Cliff would be married for life. But she left him after ten years. She had been just as certain she'd live in Santa Barbara the rest of her life. And here she was, uprooting herself and the boys after only five years.

This time is different, she told herself as she turned off Highway 101 and headed for the coast. Now, she had found her life's purpose.

Or is this also an illusion? a voice in the back of her mind whispered. She tried to ignore it. This much she knew was true—she went where the wind blew her.

Sabine found a small house to rent in Mendocino for seventy-five dollars a month. It was far smaller than their Spanish colonial in Santa Barbara, so it was a change for all of them. The house had two bedrooms. Sabine slept in the living room.

To Sabine's relief, Cliff and Fred adjusted quickly. They loved the forests and spent many happy hours playing in them. Indeed, the forests surrounding Mendocino filled them with awe. They were carpeted with ferns and the giant sequoias, unique to the California coast, loomed high overhead. Many were a thousand years old.

Little by little, their new home became a refuge for the flower children. Sabine cooked meals for them, just as she had done for the students in Santa Barbara. But this time she did it free of charge. She didn't turn any away.

155

Sabine loved the carefree atmosphere of Mendocino. As hippies flooded into town, they brought an invigorating energy. When Sabine walked down streets of the hamlet, she felt embraced. She loved the flower children's freedom and passion. They didn't just preach love and peace. They lived it. Perhaps they could change the world.

28

I Have Promised to Bring You Out of Your Misery

She spent many happy evenings at The Seagull, a village bar that was the main hippie hangout. They danced, drank, smoked, and discussed philosophy. A different local band played every night, some using handmade instruments. They played guitars, and drums like Sabine had seen in Haight-Ashbury. One guy even played on a washboard. The most rousing musician of all was Gus, the hippie guru Sabine had met in Big Sur.

Gus and Mary had recently moved away from Big Sur. Always free spirits, they split their time between Mendocino and a farm commune in Oregon. They lived wherever they pitched their teepee. Sabine welcomed Gus, Mary, and their newborn to squeeze into her small home in Mendocino.

One afternoon, Sabine was sitting in The Seagull when she overheard some farmers talking.

"It's a once-in-a-lifetime opportunity," a man said. "One hundred and forty-eight prime acres of land for forty thousand dollars! If I had the money, I'd buy it myself."

Sabine couldn't believe her ears. This was an astounding price.

"What's wrong with it?" she asked. The farmers didn't seem to mind her joining their conversation.

"Why nothing, ma'am," answered a sun-weathered man. "It's a land that sleeps. It simply hasn't been discovered yet."

"And it's too much work for the owner," said the other.

It sounded plausible, but Sabine thought there must be a catch. The price was so low! She decided to see for herself. She used the restaurant's phone to call the realtor, then headed to her truck. Carefully following the directions given her, she headed south on Highway One. She cut across Albion, a small village beside the highway, then turned left immediately before the Navarro River. A tremor of excitement shot through her as she drove up Navarro Ridge Road.

Small farms were scattered over the landscape, which soon gave way to a dense redwood forest. Once in awhile, a clearing appeared among the trees, allowing Sabine to see a steep sloping valley, and the glistening Navarro River. It was breathtaking.

Occasionally, Sabine drove by bluffs that had been cleared, where cattle roamed. After about three miles, the road branched off into a narrow trail leading to a clearing. She had reached her destination.

Sabine walked around the property in utter silence. She felt like she was on sacred ground, as if her spirit recognized the place she'd been searching for. It wasn't the most handsome landscape she'd seen. Yet she was fascinated. She knew then: *I'm going to buy this land! I'll turn it into a wonderful haven.*

A large area had been cleared—about the size of three football fields. This was strewn with massive tree stumps, remnants of ancient times. One had a diameter of six to nine feet, meaning it was at least three thousand years old! Tiny sprouts of new growth sprang up among the tree stumps.

Just then, the realtor arrived. He led Sabine through the property, heading towards a large meadow. In the middle of the meadow, a dilapidated barn was losing its battle with gravity.

"There used to be a farm here," he explained. "But apparently the farmhouse burned down long ago."

To Sabine's delight, virgin forest filled most of the land—mostly redwood, along with fir and spruce. Sabine's heart was about to leap from her. *I will buy this property!*

After returning to town, she went through the proper steps. She sought expert opinions about the land, met with a lawyer, and signed the forms. But she had made her decision walking on the property that first day.

She wasted no time, moving herself and her sons, as well as Gus, Mary, their baby onto the land.

*****

A year and a half later, Sabine was settled into her new lifestyle. She had welcomed around a dozen hippies to live with her on "The Land," the moniker they'd given the new commune. But one person didn't enjoy their new way of life. Fred found the hippie lifestyle too chaotic. One summer when the boys were in Miami with their father, he refused to come home.

"I want to stay with my dad!" he cried over the telephone. "Why did we ever leave Florida in the first place?"

He was twelve at the time. Sabine reluctantly said he could stay with his father. *It's much better that way,* she told herself. In truth, she and Fred always had trouble getting along.

159

Cliff, on the other hand, thrived on The Land, growing to be a junior hippie.

Sabine and Cliff slept in the Big House, a log cabin the hippies built out of redwood planks. It was a work in progress, but at least it had a solid foundation, four walls, a suspended ceiling, and a roof. They didn't have electricity, so they used candles and kerosene lamps at night.

The work went slower than she'd anticipated. Some of the hippies were adept at carpentry and construction. Motivating them to work, however, was another story.

Sabine and a young man named Larry were collecting stones so that he could build a fireplace before winter. She also started to decorate, giving The Big House a homey feel. She hung little bells and crocheted crosses on the walls. A young girl, one of innumerable ones who had passed through, gave Sabine the crosses. She had made them herself, attaching many to her backpack as talismans.

Sabine liked that. They needed good "vibes" in the place. She and the flower children lived in an old barn. Each night, the entire group gathered, bringing their instruments, candles, and oil lamps. They'd spend the evening hanging out, singing, drinking, and smoking. Sabine had tried repeatedly to keep them from using hashish and pot. But they always brought drugs onto The Land anyway. And if she started enforcing a bunch of rules, she thought she'd drive them away.

They lived together as one big family. However, even though she and Cliff lived with the hippies, Sabine realized early on she wasn't one herself. She didn't feel like one of them. For one thing, when everyone went naked on The Land in the summer, she didn't. Not anymore.

They needed to learn what order meant. Even though she

had changed in many ways, her father's principles stayed with her. Sabine thought that seeing one another fully exposed was unseemly. She had experienced nudity in Big Sur as a liberation. Now, she felt that taking off her clothes was abandoning part of her dignity.

Not that she would have felt ashamed, being naked before the others. But on the commune, she wanted to convey a measure of authority. She couldn't do that with no clothes on.

In many ways, Sabine carried responsibility for her hippies. She wanted to be an example of what it meant to live a responsible life. From the former millionaire, a hippie-mother was born.

She loved the ones who lived on her land, but sometimes they troubled her—like when she saw fresh examples of their drug taking.

One day, she had asked them to clear some brush. Instead, she found several sitting in the sun, passing around the pipe. She confronted them, once again. But afterwards, despair overwhelmed her. *Was this all a waste of time?* She fled down a trail into the forest. As she walked, she wrestled with the problems. *Why can't I lead these hippies to true life?* she questioned. *And what does it even look like, this true life?*

She realized now that her own life was definitely not ideal. *So, what is the truth?*

Eventually, she returned to the clearing and the Big House. She had far more questions than answers, but she wasn't willing to give up. Not yet.

She worked hard every day, doing the hard work of maintaining the property. By night she was exhausted. All she wanted to do was collapse into bed. But that wasn't easy. Her bed stood in the middle of the one large room of the Big

House—the place where the hippies gathered nightly, laughing and singing. She couldn't throw them out of the room. They were her guests.

Setting any boundaries was a big problem. Certainly, the hippies respected and loved her. When she asked, they were always willing to help with the work. However, if anyone showed them limits, it went against everything they believed in. Hippies wanted to live free from rules–a freedom Sabine increasingly began to view as a burden.

One night as the party continued in full swing, she crawled into bed in the midst of it all. They didn't seem to get the hint, continuing to laugh, sing, and play music into the wee hours around her bed. Sabine's exhausted body was crying out for sleep.

Desperate for some way to tune it all out, Sabine closed her eyes and imagined she was a queen. *Queens are accompanied by music when they go to bed. I'm just a hippie-queen.* At some point, she fell into exhausted slumber.

She didn't hear her guests leave that night. But it must have been several hours later when she startled awake to see a shadowy figure standing by her bed. It took a moment to recognize Phil, one of the hippies.

Suddenly, he began singing. "Sabine," he sang softly, without any panic, "The barn is burning…."

29

No One Does Good, Not Even One

I t took a minute for Sabine to comprehend his words. All at once, they hit her. She leaped out of bed and flew to the window. "Oh, no!"

The sky was a strange crimson. The barn stood ablaze, completely engulfed. Sabine hurriedly threw on a coat and ran outside.

When she reached the fire, she was relieved to see all of the hippies who slept in the barn had made it out safely. They stood in silence, the reflection of the flames dancing in their eyes.

They were definitely too late to save the barn. The fire was roaring, ravenously consuming the structure. Then Sabine heard a sound. The barn was moaning. *Just like the throes of death*, she thought.

Although hot air from the inferno swirled all around, a cold chill ran down her spine. "It's so eerie..." she whispered, staring into the flames. She thought of another fire long ago, when flames ate away the Kleppel mansion.

Just then, a burning beam fell in an almost upright position, stopping when it hit a crossbar. For a moment, it looked like a giant, blazing cross. Then the barn collapsed in on itself.

"Did you all see that?" Sabine said.

"Fire cleanses everything," Gus answered. "No power in the world can withstand it." He was sitting on the grass in a lotus position, as if meditating.

Sabine looked around at the silent group she had come to know and love so much. She could see they were all in awe. Most of them, like her, were not religious. Yet she suspected they felt like she did. Surely a higher power was involved here.

Sabine sank onto the grass. The fire continued to rage, but she knew it would be pointless, if not dangerous to try and put it out. All they could do was watch it burn.

John and Linda Bilderbach sat beside her on the grass. They lived in a commune in Mendocino, but often they stayed as guests on The Land. Sabine was always glad to see them. They pitched in eagerly, helping to build the houses.

Now as they sat watching the flames, Sabine thought about John and Linda. The first time they came to her property, she knew they were Christians. They constantly spoke about Jesus, and always in a way that made him sound like a good friend. John carried a small Bible with him at all times. He'd bring it out or quote from it at every possible opportunity. Even Linda constantly had Bible verses on the tip of her tongue.

Sabine smiled quietly to herself. No matter what the circumstance, these two could relate it to something from the Old or New Testament. When the food was good, John thanked his God. "He grants each his meat in due season," he'd say. When something worked out well for Linda, she'd give out a loud, "Hallelujah!"

And here was what Sabine found especially amusing. Linda

thought Jesus was the original hippie!

As the fire disintegrated into a huge pile of hot coals, Sabine thought how she liked them. But when she saw Linda or John in deep conversation with the hippies, it made her uncomfortable. *The last thing I need is a bunch of people getting saved,* she thought.

John and Linda began to sing, breaking the night's silence. "Amazing grace, how sweet the sound...." They sang softly at first, then a little louder. "...that saved a wretch like me."

Sabine sat listening, her eyes still on the burning coals. *They sound like angels,* she thought.

"I once was lost, but now am found." Their voices pierced the cold night air. One by one, the rest joined in, mostly humming, their eyes still riveted on the fire. "'Twas blind, but now I see."

Was I also lost? The thought pierced Sabine's mind.... *Am I lost?*

She gazed into the fire, shaking the nonsense away. John and Linda continued singing, one Christian song after the other. The others ran to get their instruments. Gus played on his homemade bass fiddle, fashioned from a bucket. Some played guitar, others rattled spoons, while still others beat on makeshift drums.

When Jesus or other Bible things from the songs hit Sabine's mind, she kept them at bay. *Tonight, I'll just enjoy the melodies and not pay attention to the lyrics.*

On the morning after the fire, Sabine surveyed the destruction. Some of the embers still glowed red hot, including what was left of the redwood stumps by the barn. Wisps of smoke curled from the blackened beam lying in a mound of ashes. Sabine realized the large amounts of wood they had stored for winter had fueled the fire even more.

Sabine's eyes ran over the ash heap, as she remembered. Before they built the big house, Sabine and her sons had lived in the barn. The loft where she'd slept was completely demolished. Gus had built it for her, directly over the goat stable. She'd only been able to reach it by ladder. On the timber flooring, she had laid out the Persian rug she brought from Santa Barbara.

She huddled deeper into her jacket. *This is also the place where I experimented with LSD. Just that one time.*

Sabine had wanted to experience what fascinated her hippies so much. But Sabine honestly thought LSD wouldn't affect her. Soon, however, she had begun to laugh maniacally. Her mind skipped over the pain she had faced—Fred moving to Miami, losing Hans, even her broken marriage. And somehow it was all hysterically funny.

After that evening, she hated drugs even more.

Now as she tramped around the charred rubble, she thought how much drugs had destroyed their community. It was far worse than the fire last night. In just eighteen months, many of the hippies had withdrawn into themselves, sitting alone, always high, vanishing into another world.

Her eyes fell on something in the ashes—remnants of books. They'd kept their library in the barn. All the books the hippies had brought to The Land must have burned—titles by Kafka, Camus, Hesse, and Marx. Then she saw what was left of a Bible and beside it, a small metal crucifix in the ashes. She had never seen either before, and wondered who had left them in the barn library. Carefully, she picked the cross from the warm ashes, then the Bible. It disintegrated at her first touch, trickling through her fingers like dust. A gust of wind suddenly came up, blowing ashes across the clearing. Sabine looked down and saw one shred of the burnt Bible remained in her fingers. She read the fragment: "They are all gone out of the way, they are together become unprofitable; there is none that doeth good, no, not one."

What does that mean? That doesn't apply to me, does it? Sabine thought. Didn't she do good? If anyone did good, it was her—the hippie-mother.

Then it struck her. Last night was Halloween. The barn had gone up in flames on the evening when according to old beliefs, spirits traveled through... The Land!

30

Out of the Depths I Cry to You

Sabine shook off her ridiculous ideas and headed for the Big House. *I'm getting far too superstitious.*

A few days later, the police solved the mystery of what caused the fire. It was the same arsonist who had burned a hotel in a nearby town. He was a hippie who struggled with pyromania. Sabine remembered: He had been a guest on her land the night of the fire.

The police made another discovery while investigating the fire. One of them motioned Sabine over to the garden, not far from the burned-out barn. He walked to a row of plants and ripped off a stalk. "You need to get rid of these," he said, showing her a stem with seven pointed leaves. Someone had been growing marijuana right in her garden!

It was another sign to Sabine. Her experiment of taking hippies away from the city to get them off drugs had failed.

Sabine had to admit even more than that. She had left everything behind, yet she hadn't found meaning for her life. Even in the life of a hippie-mother. She wanted something more.

*****

Sabine shivered in excitement as her jet readied for takeoff. She was embarking on a new journey, one that would take her to the far ends of the earth. The Lufthansa 747 powered down the runway, then lifted heavily from the San Francisco runway. It was January, 22, 1971.

Sabine watched out her porthole as the plane climbed through the clouds. She could scarcely believe she was headed to India and Nepal! But first, she'd stop in Germany for a brief visit with Father. It had been ten years since her mother's death, and he was living alone in the same apartment.

She twisted in her coach class seat, trying not to brush elbows with the man seated next to her. *At least I'm getting away from the hippies,* she thought. She hated to admit it, but a side benefit of this trip was getting away from them.

It was almost two years since she had bought The Land, opening it up to the hippies. Now they were really getting on her nerves. Not only was she unable to persuade them not to use drugs. She couldn't teach them anything! *Why have I even bothered?* she asked herself.

The last straw was when they ate up all the apricot jam she'd preserved last summer. She had made herself very clear. They were saving that jam for winter. But by the end of summer, they had devoured every golden jar.

That was when something inside Sabine snapped. Now all she felt was frustration. She was growing increasingly desperate for something—but what it was, she didn't know. Perhaps she'd find what her heart was crying out for in the East.

From Germany, Sabine would travel to Asia by train. By this point, many thousands were heading east on "the hippie trail"–not just those who had dropped out of society, but students, intellectuals, even rock stars, and movie actors. For most of the journey, Sabine would go overland. She was seeking what all the other travelers sought–enlightenment.

Recently, Sabine had grown curious about India. She'd read many books, and in San Francisco, she had visited ashrams–spiritual centers where gurus taught their disciples. They intrigued her.

It was as if they lived their lives in slow motion. Even the atmosphere in the ashrams carried a sense of mystery. The followers went about barefoot, gliding softly over carpets and other woven materials that cushioned their footsteps. It was absolutely quiet. No one spoke. And when they did, it was quietly, a few words merely breathed. Indian music played in the background, airy and haunting with sitars and wooden flutes.

Despite all this, Sabine hadn't experienced anything particularly spiritual at the ashrams. But the Indians she'd met did impress her. At times, they appeared high, but without drugs. They said they'd experienced enlightenment. They had found truth.

At one ashram, they'd spoken in reverent tones about a Tibetan monk named Thubten Yeshe. The more she heard, the more Sabine felt she should seek him out. He lived in a mountain monastery close to Kathmandu, in Nepal.

And so here she was, embarking on this journey. She was traveling very light. Her only baggage was a soft duffel in the overhead compartment. It held a sleeping mat, a baggy gown made from a gunnysack, and a gray cape she had stitched from a U.S. Army blanket.

When she landed in Frankfurt, an old friend, Monique and

her husband met the plane. They took Sabine to her father's apartment in Dusseldorf. Hans was away in university, but it was good to see Father. He was still tall, though his back was bent and he looked a lot leaner.

As they sat next to one another, sipping strong coffee, an unspoken sadness hung over them. She glanced at Mother's picture on a small desk.

Sabine put her cup on the coffee table. "I haven't told you the real reason I'm going to the East, Father."

He waited quietly.

"I'm traveling to a monastery, to see a great teacher."

Father put his cup beside hers. "It's a good thing, looking for truth." Then he put his arms around her and hugged her, like she was a little girl again. "And it's good that you're searching for it in the simple life."

With that, Walter Koritke gave his blessing for his daughter's quest. Her truth-seeking venture to Asia. She knew it sounded strange to him, but he preferred this to her life in high society.

At the train station, he wrapped his arms around her once more, kissing her soundly on both cheeks. Then Sabine climbed aboard the eastbound train.

On the 29th of January, she reached Istanbul. She was among thousands—mostly young people—who were on similar pilgrimages to the East. She was glad she'd decided to come this way. She had enough money to fly, but taking a jet to a monastery sounded contradictory.

But now, as she wedged herself into a rickety Turkish bus, she was having second thoughts. The vehicle probably dated back to World War II! She'd have to travel thousands of miles on similar vehicles, stopping along the way in local inns, wherever she could lay her head.

Her thoughts turned to alarm when the bus driver began to race through mountain passes at top speed. He passed other drivers on blind curves, and veered dangerously close to steep drop-offs, inches away from where the pavement ended. *He has a death wish!* she thought, clutching the duffel on her lap. When she dared to look down as they careened around one curve, she saw the rusting wreckage of a bus that hadn't made it, lying hundreds of feet below. She held her breath as they rounded each perilous turn.

*****

In coming weeks, she learned that Iranian and Pakistani drivers shared the same suicidal tendencies. On her long journey eastward, she made friends with a young Canadian named John. He decided to travel with Sabine, to make sure she was safe.

However, their trip almost came to an abrupt end in Karachi.

One afternoon, she and John were walking through the city. The smell of strange spices and fruits in the market mingled with the odor of cooking fires and crowds of people. Just before they crossed a street, a Pakistani man collapsed right in front of them, crying out in pain. His face contorted into a death grimace as he lay in the gutter, convulsing.

"This man needs help!" she yelled before bending over him. Before she could touch him, some men dressed in white dashed at Sabine from behind a fruit stand. Pinning her arms to her sides, they cried wildly, "No touch! No touch!"

Did they stop her because she was a woman? Or perhaps, because they believed it was this man's fate to die? There was no one to explain. But within minutes, the man stopped convulsing, growing silent at her feet. Then death overtook him.

In shock, Sabine and John returned to their hotel, only to discover a Pakistani man they'd befriended had stolen their money for the ferry to Bombay!

Fortunately, a kind American couple paid for Sabine and John's ferry tickets. But the whole experience left a bitter taste in her mouth. Evidently, not everyone in the East had found enlightenment.

31

The Fool Says in his Heart, "There is no God."

With relief, Sabine boarded the ferry to Bombay, India, where she and John parted ways. After a few days in Bombay, Sabine left on a hopelessly overfilled train. Not only were people packed into every seat. They also sat in the aisles. Some even rode on top of the train.

She rode for days, sweating and sticking to the seat. It was not a pleasant ride. All her romantic notions of making an overland pilgrimage evaporated in the scorching heat.

After twelve days, she reached Patna on the Ganges River. It was the 23rd of March. She was completely exhausted. She abandoned her original plans and bought a ticket on a plane for Kathmandu.

She should've known a domestic Indian airline would be in similar condition to Asian buses and trains. As the eight-passenger plane made its shaky assent into the sky, sheer terror ran through Sabine. She breathed a sigh of relief when the decrepit little plane made a safe landing in the foothills of the Himalayas.

Taking a deep breath of the cool mountain air, she was glad to be on the final part of her trip. Plunging into the crowded streets of Kathmandu, she admired the women's saris in sapphire, magenta, and lime green. Holy men passed in scarlet robes. Everyone looked as if the winter wind had turned their skin to leather.

As she made her way through the labyrinth of lanes, she passed temples and shrines. So many gods! Every few yards was another shrine, usually with a person or two praying before it. Some of the shrines were shaped like a pagoda, with giant eyes painted on the roof. Sabine thought, *These people must live their lives on a spiritual plane.*

Sabine asked fellow travelers how to get to Yeshe's monastery. She boarded another dilapidated bus and found her way outside the town to a white-washed building on the side of a hill. Dozens of Tibetan prayer flags on the roof–cloth pennants in various colors–fluttered in the thin air.

This is the place! she thought. *Here I will find what I've been searching for.*

It was not to be.

Sabine spent three months at the monastery, from April to the end of June. They kept to a simple diet of rice, vegetables, and water. This was supposed to free the mind for a transcendental experience.

She quickly adjusted to the schedule, including five hours a day in meditation. She sat cross-legged on the floor with other students and tried to clear her mind.

"You must think of nothing, absolutely nothing," the teacher said at the first session. "You feel complete emptiness in yourselves... nothing moves you... nothing... nothing...."

For Sabine, this was more easily said than done. She closed

her eyes and tried to think of nothing. Instead she found her mind wandering. She thought of the man dying in the gutter in Karachi. She thought about the petrifying bus rides through the mountains of Asia. She thought of the jars of apricot jam the hippies had emptied. She thought of how tired she was of eating rice.

Above all, she thought how much her back and rear end ached! She hadn't recovered from the weeks of travel, getting to the monastery. Her back hurt more with each meditation session.

However, as the weeks passed, she was able to curb her thoughts a little. She repeated the mantra, *om*. Even though she was unable to think of *nothing*, she was able to think of *almost nothing*.

During the five hours of meditating, the students were expected to stay in the lotus position with their backs absolutely straight. When Sabine's shoulders fell forward or her spine relaxed even a little, the teacher came from behind and shoved her in the back.

However, Sabine's worst times were spent listening to other students tell about wonderful experiences that happened during meditation. *What's wrong with me?* She wasn't like these people. She was trying as hard as she could to receive some insight… anything! But no matter how hard she tried, she couldn't make herself feel anything out of the ordinary. Certainly nothing mystical.

When she finally got to meet Thubten Yeshe, it was anticlimactic. He was a nice enough man. He spoke soft words that hinted of great meaning. But Sabine was disappointed.

As each week passed, her frustration grew. Finally, she couldn't take it anymore. After three months of meditation, rice, and water, she left the monastery. It was another defeat. Her pilgrimage was a failure.

She flew home via New Delhi, and London. On the plane headed for California, she thought how useless it had all been. Struggling to get comfortable in the coach section, Sabine had to admit it. She had traveled to the ends of the earth and come home empty-handed. It was all for nothing. She closed her eyes. *There is no truth to find.*

The cold realization settled over her. Life was meaningless, after all. A black void. And what about God? *He doesn't exist either.* In all of her travels and searching, she hadn't found him.

She didn't know what to do next. Maybe she should sell The Land and move to Canada? Live a life of solitude. She no longer believed she could make a difference in the world. She was powerless to help that dying man in Karachi. And she certainly hadn't been able to make a difference in the lives of the hippies.

The flight attendant moved through the plane, reminding everyone to fasten their seatbelts. They were landing.

When Sabine made it home, she saw that her son Cliff now towered over her. He grinned and bent down, allowing her to kiss him on the cheek.

The hippies rushed out when she arrived at The Land. They gathered her in a huge, group hug. She felt a little better. That night as she collapsed into her bed in the Big House, she thought, *Maybe I won't leave after all. Not right away.*

32

I Am The Way and The Truth and The Life

In coming days, Sabine saw how things had changed on The Land. The biggest difference was in Gus. While she'd been gone, John and Linda had apparently pushed him over the edge. He said he'd "committed his life to Christ." Now Gus was wild about Jesus, too, and like John, was constantly quoting Bible verses. It drove her crazy!

It wasn't only Gus. Sabine was dismayed to find others in her commune had become Christians as well. They all carried big Bibles. They called themselves "Jesus People."

This is the last thing I need, she thought.

Another change was, Gus was alone in his teepee. Sabine was shocked to learn Mary had left him, taking their baby daughter with her. It wasn't because of his conversion, either. He had been unfaithful.

Gus told Sabine how it happened. They were staying at the Lighthouse in Eureka, a Christian commune, when Gus fell for another girl. "When Mary found out I slept with her, she left me," Gus said, sounding sad and ashamed.

"Nice conversion," Sabine snapped. "Here you are preaching to people about their sins, and you cheat on your wife? The mother of your child?"

Gus hung his head. "What I did was wrong. I'm still full of sin. But Sabine, you're not free either. You've got to ask God for forgiveness."

"Sin, sin, sin! Can't you talk about anything else?"

She missed the old Gus. For a few weeks, Sabine watched him. The new Gus was fired up. He was always saying how free he was. But his behavior did not fit with his words. How could he talk about love and faithfulness and betray Mary?

Sabine thought she knew the answer. He was a flighty sort, jumping onto every new bandwagon. He never stuck with anything long. Like most hippies, he showed no consistency and hardly any reliability. He would soon tire of his Christianity.

Nevertheless, his Bible euphoria irked her. Especially his non-stop tongue wagging about guilt, forgiveness, and new beginnings.

Early the following spring, Sabine moved into a small, new house on the edge of the clearing. The hippies had worked for months, building it for her. They wanted to show appreciation for all she'd done for them. It was charming. They had crafted the entire house completely of old redwood. From the foundation to the roof, they didn't use a single nail. It even had a stone fireplace. They named the cottage, the Wood Butcher.

Cliff was eighteen now and had a girlfriend. He decided to live at the Big House with the others. So, Sabine had the new little cabin to herself.

Sabine loved having her own space. No longer would she have to try to sleep while hippies partied around her bed.

By this time, The Land was home to around fifty people.

Numbers fluctuated because of their transient, free-spirited ways. One of the regulars was Tommy. He, too, had recently converted to Christianity.

Originally, Tommy voiced loud protests against the "Jesus freaks" on The Land. He had even taken to studying the Bible, so that he could discredit their beliefs. Repeatedly, he took a Bible into the forest, seeking a quiet place to read it and find contradictions.

It was there in the forest that he'd become convinced. The Bible was the true Word of God. He decided to put his faith in Jesus. Tommy joined the Jesus People, who continued to annoy Sabine with their constant preaching.

"It's the truth, Sabine. It's the truth," Tommy told her one afternoon. They were sitting together on a bench in the sunshine.

"Oh Tommy, now even you have gone crazy," Sabine sighed.

"But Sabine, do you know the Bible at all?"

Her heart skipped a beat. "No, I guess I don't. There's a lot I don't understand."

"May I explain it to you?" He smiled.

She had walked right into his trap! Sabine tried to think how to get out of this situation. She didn't want to hurt his feelings. Yet she feared she wouldn't be able to oppose his arguments. He was a skilled debater. She'd heard him argue persuasively on many subjects.

On the other hand, was there any harm in learning more about the Bible? She just had to stand really firm in what she believed, and not let herself get carried away.

"Okay. Tell me something about the Bible," she said, adding, "But don't you dare try to convert me!"

She agreed to give him seven days. Tommy came to her little

wooden home each day and sat reading the Bible with her, cross-legged on the floor.

"The Bible is the Word of God," he began on the first afternoon. "It shows us the way to God."

"The way to God? If he exists at all, there are many ways to him. More than one pathway can lead to the same destination," Sabine answered, somewhat defiantly. She adjusted the cushion she was sitting on.

Since her disastrous trip to India, she doubted more and more that there was a God. And if he did exist, she was certain he wasn't the Christian God. She believed each religion held a grain of truth, one key to the big mystery.

Tommy didn't seem to notice her objections. He was quiet a long time. And when he spoke, he didn't argue.

He said softly, "Sabine, I don't have all the answers. I can only tell you about the joy that has filled my heart. The way Jesus has changed my life."

Sabine looked past Tommy out the window. It was a blustery day. Branches on the redwoods thrashed in the wind.

Tommy leafed through his Bible. "Sabine," he said, "Jesus *is* the truth, the truth in person."

A torrential rage flooded Sabine. She didn't know what angered her more–Tommy and his zeal, or Jesus who claimed to be the only truth!

She could embrace most Christian ideas. Loving one's neighbor appealed to her. She found the Sermon on the Mount brilliant. Even the Ten Commandments were necessary. We couldn't live well without them. Theft, for example, must be forbidden. She remembered how angry she'd been when the hippies ate all her apricot jam.

However, this notion of Jesus being the only truth, excluding

181

all other religions…. It was intolerance, claiming other religions were false, that Jesus was the only way to God…. That bothered her the most.

"What does Jesus base his claim on?" she shot at Tommy, more sharply than she intended.

"He doesn't give a reason. At least not with words." Tommy sounded calm and confident. He was silent a moment, looking out the window. "Jesus didn't back up his claim with arguments. He showed he was God by the things he did. By miracles. And especially, by dying for us. He died for all of us, including you, Sabine. If I'm truly honest, I don't completely understand it all myself. I'm still learning. But in my heart, I know it's true."

Sabine didn't say anything. Tommy's words just hung there. Then with one hand, he held his Bible. With the other, his finger traced the cross on its cover. He looked at Sabine again and she saw tears in his eyes.

"Sabine, do you know what the greatest love is? No one loves more than the one who gives his life for his friends. That's what the New Testament says in John fifteen, verse thirteen. And that's exactly what Jesus did for all of us. He's offering you this precious gift, Sabine. The gift of his own life."

Sabine felt confused. She listened to the wind rushing outside the cabin. It was all so overwhelming. She didn't know what she believed anymore. Could this be the truth she had searched for? Was it in the Bible all along? Had it all been decided on the cross? Did God's Son really die for her… as a friend?

Tommy was silent, waiting for her.

33

Jesus Is Lord

Sabine saw it clearly. Indifference wasn't an option. The Christian faith was either based on a lie–in which case she could forget about Jesus and not worry—or it was the truth. And if it was true, she'd have to embrace it wholeheartedly. She couldn't sit on the fence. She had to make a decision, a decision that would be life-changing.

She sighed. Part of her wanted to rip Tommy's Bible out of his hands and throw it into the fireplace. Yet she couldn't. It had captured her.

Tommy left, and Sabine wished she hadn't agreed to six more days. But she and Tommy continued to meet. Their conversations were intense, just like on the first day. Each time Tommy left, Sabine went prowling around The Land and into the forest. She was torn.

At night, she'd thrash around in her bed, unable to sleep. Her mind raced. These were the most difficult seven days of her life. No matter what she did, trying to go about her normal work, she couldn't concentrate. Over and over, she thought of Tommy's words: *No one loves more than the one who gives his life for his friends.* The words repeated in her mind every waking moment.

On the seventh day, neither Tommy nor Sabine said much. Once again they sat in front of the window on the floor of her cottage, watching the redwood trees rustling in the gentle breeze. Then Tommy said something that shocked her. "Sabine, you're in the dark."

Sabine reared up. *What an insult! Who does he think he think he is?* At twenty-six, he knew far less than she did at forty-six. In fact, she could have been his mother.

"Tommy, look me in the eyes and say that once more!"

"You're in the dark, Sabine," he said once more, quietly yet firmly. His eyes looked right through her. He was clear, convinced.

To Sabine's shock, she changed. In an instant, her heart was different. Without knowing exactly how or why, she *knew* what Tommy had been sharing with her all week was true. She *believed.* It was as if she'd been blind all her life, and now suddenly she could see… everything around her… with absolute clarity.

Giant tears filled her eyes, spilling down her cheeks. She had tried so hard, for so many years to find the truth. But everything she'd tried had come to nothing. She had been fighting against the real truth, this very Man on the Cross.

"He died for you, Sabine. All you need to do is accept his gift." Tommy's voice was gentle.

She felt it. God was giving her an amazing gift, with no strings attached. No language in the world could express what she was feeling at this moment. All she could do was cry. And as the tears streamed down her face, for the first time in her life she called out to God. She sobbed, "My God. My God," over and over.

She poured out her heart, surrendering the restless impatience that had driven her. It had been almost obsessive–a hopeless search for a fulfilling life. As she cried, she felt the accumulated guilt of years lifting from her. It was as if her tears were washing it all away. Tommy handed her a tissue box.

Sabine took a deep breath. For the first time in her life, she felt free. A sweet, warm peace enveloped her.

Sabine and Tommy continued to sit together with their eyes closed and heads bowed. *God has given everything for me!* Sabine thought. It was so amazing. A deep love welled up and she felt a reverence for God she'd never known.

Before she finished, she whispered one more promise to God. "No matter what I do, from now on I will serve you with all my heart."

She didn't realize it yet, but everything would change. This was the beginning of a life that was more enthralling, more fulfilling, and more challenging than she could have imagined.

Was this just another fad for Sabine? Was she riding the Jesus wave, just as she rode the high society wave, the Fritz Perls wave, and even the India wave? No. Sabine knew this was different. Completely different. She really was a new person. In all of her years, through all her seeking, nothing had struck her as deeply as this encounter with Jesus Christ. The Man on the Cross was her friend.

Tommy finally left, but her tears kept coming. She had never felt like this. Nothing had ever felt so *right*.

She remembered Jim Durken. He often came from Eureka to hold Bible studies on The Land. He said, "You can completely rely on God. He's dependable, completely different than people are."

When Sabine heard him say that, it annoyed her. Now, those words overwhelmed her. She felt a peace she couldn't explain.

*****

The next time Jim came back, she told him about it. They were walking through the redwood forest when Sabine told Jim,"I feel such a peace now. It's like my entire soul has quieted."

They sat on a giant tree stump to rest. Jim said, "Over a thousand years ago, Augustine had the same experience. He said our hearts stay restless until they find rest in him. Sabine, you have found the rest Augustine was talking about."

Sabine smiled, feeling the warmth of the sun on her face. "For the first time, I feel I've arrived. I've found what I was looking for. For so long." She searched for words, then said, "I'm home."

The truth settled over her. She hadn't felt at home since she'd left her parents' house in Königsberg, so many years ago. For decades she had been constantly seeking, never satisfied. She wanted more. More than millions of dollars. More than a simple life in her own house. More than a religious experience. And yes, more than ideals that turn out to be illusions.

She'd found something that satisfied the yearning. But it was more than that. She had found God. And in finding him, she had finally found herself.

Jim continued to come and teach at The Land. The stories he taught from the Bible enthralled Sabine. Saul, who killed many Christians, became Paul, the first missionary. Martha, an ordinary woman who worked all the time, neglected the most important thing—listening to Jesus. How fascinating that Martha's sister, who neglected work to sit at Jesus' feet, was held up as the role model!

Sabine soaked in Jim's teachings, as well as studying the Word of God on her own. This led to her being honest for the first time about her marriage to Cliff. For so long, she'd blamed him for their divorce, especially his alcoholism. Now, she knew. She also bore responsibility for their breakup. She had tried to be the perfect wife, but she had shamed Cliff, despising him for his imperfection. Over and over, she made sure he felt her scorn. She saw that she had driven him further into alcoholism.

Jim taught that Jesus' death paid the penalty for all their sins. By accepting his forgiveness, these sins were wiped away. Sabine believed this. But she also knew she could not rest until she asked Cliff for forgiveness.

What should she do? Call him? No, that was too impersonal. Should she write a letter? That was too distant. She had to talk to him face to face.

The next day, she went to the bank. She discovered only five hundred dollars was left in her savings. She spent most of it, booking a trip to Miami.

Before she left, she called him. Cliff, who had long since remarried, sounded completely shocked to hear her voice. "After all this time, what could you possibly want from me? If it's money, I'll not give you another penny!"

When Sabine assured him she didn't want money, he blustered. "There's no chance of us getting back together!"

The rest of their phone conversation went badly. Still, Sabine knew she had to see him in person.

And so, on a warm Miami afternoon, Sabine stood outside Cliff's house. A nervous chill swept over her. She had second thoughts. Why was she putting herself through this? What was the point in seeing Cliff again?

However, she'd come too far to go back now. Summoning her courage, she marched up the footpath and rang the bell.

34

Confess Your Sins and Pray for Each Other So That You May be Healed

A much older Cliff opened the door and stood there stiffly. "Do come in."

Sabine tried not to stare. He looked so different–the years had not been kind.

Politely, he led her into the living room, and offered her a cup of tea. When they sat facing each other, Cliff looked her in the eye. "Now, tell me why you're really here."

"I just had to see you, Cliff," she started. "I'm a Christian now. My life has changed."

He didn't react, didn't say a word.

"As part of this, I'm here to ask for your forgiveness," she continued. "Do you understand, Cliff? I always blamed you for everything. I... I hated you. But in reality, I gave you no chance. I made it impossible for you to stop drinking. In fact, I pushed you further into it."

Cliff sat silently in his armchair, his face expressionless. After a long while he said, "Well Sabine, I don't know what to say." He looked at her blankly, then asked, "Are you on drugs?"

She shook her head.

"I'm not sure what to make of your religious delusion."

Sabine smiled at him, "Look at me Cliff. I'm not deluded. And I'm not on drugs. I'm happier than I've ever been. I've found the truth!"

Cliff scratched his head and nodded politely. She could tell he didn't know what to make of what she said.

"I've asked God for forgiveness. Cliff, do you think you can forgive me, too?"

"What did you say?"

"Can you forgive me? For all the things I did to you?"

"But...." Cliff's face was a map of confusion. "Well, if it makes you feel better. I forgive you. Okay?"

"It's important to me. I had to talk with you about it."

"It's okay. I... understand," he said. But she could tell he didn't.

Her time with Fred went much better. It was good to see how much her son had grown, and how well he was doing in school.

As her taxi pulled away, Sabine knew she had made the right decision to come.

After she returned from Miami, a telephone call from Germany brought devastating news. "Your father is dying," her cousin said. The doctors guessed he had a few days, at best.

Tears streamed down Sabine's face. She was losing her beloved father. And she didn't have the money to fly to his bedside.

In a daze, she hung up the phone, and ran out of the cabin, onto the clearing. A group of hippies standing there saw she was crying. "It's my father, he's dying," Sabine said before breaking down completely. Word spread throughout the commune. Soon most of the Jesus People had gathered with her to pray and wait for further news.

Sabine was touched when they refused to leave, spending the entire night with her. It would have been far worse to wait alone. In the wee hours of the morning, the phone rang again.

Sabine's hands shook as she held the phone. She replaced the receiver and surrendered to new tears. He was gone. She had lost the one she could always count on. He had never failed to give her honest counsel. Her loss was a dull pain in her chest. She missed him so deeply, and it was only the first day. She knew she'd miss him until the end of her days.

Then the worst thought crowded out everything else. *I wasn't able to tell Father about Jesus. If only he hadn't died so soon! Now it's too late.*

Later that morning, she walked alone through The Land. Her heart was heavy with grief. At the same time, a comfort flowed into her soul. *I have the Father God to turn to.* It amazed her that the God of the universe cared so deeply for her. He knew the pain she was feeling.

Then she thought how Jesus had spent his entire life, then gave his life to save others. Sabine decided. *That's how I want to live from now on.*

Already, in the few weeks since her conversion, her life had changed so much. How could she had have lived so long without knowing Jesus? From now on, she would serve him and be a friend to others.

Tension was growing on The Land. Things had changed so radically, and not everyone was happy about it. For instance, they prayed before every meal. They had Bible study almost every evening. And wherever you went on the commune,

191

you could hear someone loudly singing praise songs. For the hippies who hadn't converted, all this Jesus stuff was just too much.

Big changes were happening in Sabine, too. As she continued to study the Bible, she changed her mind about certain things. Things she used to think of as innocent. Like nudity, for example. In the past she thought being naked was freeing. Now she regretted embracing it so wholeheartedly.

Maybe it's good to be ashamed of nakedness, she thought one day as she walked through the clearing. That's one way God shows how precious we are. We're humans, not animals. We have a dignity we should cherish.

Just then, she came across one of the hippies stretched out on the grass—as naked as the day he was born. She called out the first thing that came to her mind. "Hey, Johnny! God even gave Adam and Eve clothes. Put something on!"

She laughed at how surprised he looked. He quickly pulled a blanket over himself.

Some found the Christian behavior and new rules intolerable. They left the commune. But Sabine was firm. It was time God's rules were put in place on The Land. If people left, so be it. She saw now, how important boundaries were for group living.

However, she was surprised and saddened when her son Cliff left. He had been willing to follow his mother to a hippie commune. But he couldn't accept her becoming a Christian. He felt confused, and perhaps a little betrayed. Since he was old enough to make his own decisions, he and his girlfriend moved to another commune.

Although many left, other hippies continued to arrive in even larger numbers. She turned no one away, even when The

Land's population swelled to more than a hundred.

One evening after supper in the Big House, they came to a general consensus. They didn't want to call the property The Land anymore. Someone said, "Let's call it The Lord's Land!"

"Hallelujah!" Gus exclaimed in agreement.

Sabine liked it, too. "Lots of us have given our lives to God. I think it's wonderful to commit our land to him, too."

So it was settled.

The next morning, a few set to work carving and painting a big sign. By the end of the day, they placed it near the entrance. Anyone driving by on Navarro Ridge Road could see it plainly: "The Lord's Land."

The new sign was literally that–a sign that Sabine had given herself and everything she owned to God. She had invested her entire fortune in this property. Now it belonged entirely to God.

A new fire began to burn in Sabine. She told anyone who would listen, "I'm on fire for Jesus!" She felt like she was smiling all the time.

Sabine adopted a new habit of walking about the property each afternoon, pouring her heart out to her Savior. At first, it felt strange talking to God—almost like talking to herself. Then she became used to it. It was such a comfort to send little messages to God, even about the most ordinary details.

For example, if somebody said it was a splendid day, in her mind she'd send up a little thank you. Or perhaps, ask him to send rain for the vegetables in the garden. It continued to amaze her—the God who created the entire world was interested in the smallest aspects of her life.

Like other believers on The Lord's Land, Sabine found a good church to join. Her pastor and his wife modeled the love of Jesus, especially in the way they cared for a severely handicapped, adopted daughter. It was just another way God was speaking to Sabine, showing his love that she hadn't seen before.

One afternoon as she walked through the clearing, she prayed, "Jesus, I'm so grateful you've saved me. But so many don't know you. They have no idea you exist and you love them."

She thought back to the day she'd first gone to Haight-Ashbury. She remembered speaking with the drug addicts sitting in a circle on the sidewalk. Then, her thoughts ran on to Karachi, when a man had died in the gutter, right at her feet.

"Father, who tells those people in the gutter about you? Who bends down to show them your love?"

Immediately, a voice spoke in her heart. "Why not you, Sabine?"

Her heart skipped a beat. Surely, she wasn't qualified for that. "Oh, Father God, no. I can't do that. I don't want to do that."

And yet on this quiet afternoon, she knew as surely as the sky above her was blue. It was God's gentle Spirit calling her to leave The Lord's Land, and her comfortable, familiar life. He wanted her to go help people in need. Somehow, without knowing all the details, she knew he would take her into the slums of a big city, to the poorest and neediest of people. She seemed to hear God whisper, "I love those people desperately. I want you to show them my love."

35

How Can They Hear without Someone Preaching to Them?

At first, she tried to close her ears to the quiet voice. She remembered the heavy stench that permeated the district of Haight-Ashbury and the streets of Karachi. *Besides,* she tried to rationalize to herself, *What can I offer those people?*

That very evening, Tommy announced he was taking a group from Eureka, all the way to New York City for a mission trip. And Sabine knew immediately. God was calling her to go on this trip.

She felt comfortable leaving The Lord's Land in the hands of some who had been with her a long time. She knew the commune would do fine, even without her there.

As she looked back over the years, she was amazed to see what had been accomplished. A sanctuary had emerged from deserted land. She couldn't number how many students, hippies, and dropouts they had welcomed in. They gave them a roof over their heads and nourishing food to eat, for however long they chose to stay. And now, they also told them about

Jesus, his friendship, his death on the cross, and the new life he offered.

She thought how many had chosen to believe. Sadly, she also remembered the ones who fell back into their old life of alcohol and drugs. But many remained steadfast in their new faith.

Sabine was amazed how hard these new kind of hippies worked—both in terms of their spiritual growth, as well as what they accomplished on the property and in the garden. And to her relief, they no longer grew marijuana.

In October of 1973, Sabine moved to Eureka, California, to prepare for her trip to New York. Since her goal was to work among the Puerto Ricans, she learned some basic Spanish. And she decided that from now on, she would live completely by faith. She'd trust God in everything, even with regard to money.

That's why she decided to refuse Cliff's alimony. Relinquishing her right to that money was wonderfully freeing. In fact, she had never felt so free. It was an amazing paradox: By giving up financial security, she now felt a deep peace.

She wrote Cliff, telling of her decision. "God will care for me," she told him. He didn't answer, except to immediately stop the monthly payments.

Two weeks later, it was as if God rewarded her faith. A large logging company made a sensational offer: eighty thousand dollars for the purchase of the forested hillside of her land. That was more than double the sum she had paid for the entire property. Besides, that portion of the forest was useless to their commune. Those acres were too steep to build on. That would still leave her with twenty-seven acres, including some forest.

After much prayer, as well as the advice of experts, she accepted the offer. She used the money to renovate cabins on The Lord's Land, and add electricity and water. Plus she was able to put some toward the venture in New York City.

In the spring of 1974, Sabine, Tommy, and the rest of the group—twenty-two in all—left for Brooklyn. They made quite a caravan as they drove old, battered cars more than three thousand miles across the United States.

Their first task upon arrival was to find a place to live. Sabine was pleased with what they found—a large house for five hundred dollars a month, half a block away from where most of the druggies hung out.

Sabine shared her room with four other women—three were prostitutes before finding Christ.

One night, the team brought back a young girl who was trembling all over. Sabine's heart melted the moment she saw Mary. The girl was lovely in a delicate way. Over hot cocoa, Mary's story spilled out.

Her home life had been difficult. So she had run away from her parents... directly into the arms of a pimp.

The team had found her that evening, all alone, crying pitifully on a park bench. They had urged her to come with them, but Mary was afraid her pimp would follow her. After all, she was his property. But the guys on the team refused to give up. With Mary cowering behind them, they found the pimp.

"A weasel of a man," one told Sabine. They managed to persuade him to release Mary.

Back at the rental house, Mary was too afraid to speak. But the gratitude in her eyes spoke volumes. She acted as if she felt safe around Sabine. And so, Sabine had another woman to share her bedroom with.

Everyone in the team quickly found jobs to support themselves. Sabine and Mary worked as cleaning ladies. It wasn't long before Mary also came to faith in Jesus Christ. Sabine was thrilled. Mary had a similar experience as Sabine's. Her eyes had been opened to Jesus. All at once, she could believe: "He's the Son of God, and he offers me his friendship. He died for me." Sabine knelt beside her on the floor and thanked God for this miracle.

Sabine's heart was turning cartwheels. It didn't matter that she was working as a cleaning lady, and sharing a room with four others. Living like this was such a privilege!

Her new neighborhood couldn't have been more different than living on The Lord's Land. Instead of the peace and quiet of their commune, the Brooklyn neighborhood screamed with noise. At all hours, day and night, ambulances raced down the streets. Their piercing wail reminded Sabine of the dangers lurking outside her door. Police were everywhere, and still, the neighborhood crime rate was staggering. Once, a young man was murdered directly in front of their house.

They also had to contend with robberies. They weren't immune, even though they owned little of value. One time their house was broken into when everyone was gone except for a team member named Tomas. He surprised the thieves. They all ran away except for one, whom Tomas was able to catch. To the young man's astonishment, Tomas invited him to sit and have some coffee and cake. Confused and stammering, the would-be thief accepted a quick snack before leaving as soon as he could.

They never saw him again, but Sabine wondered if this encounter changed him.

"God only knows," Tomas said with a grin.

36

You Will be My Witnesses…to the Ends of the Earth

The unlikely group of missionaries began to establish their presence in the community. Once a week, they treated junkies to dinner in a rented hall.

During these months, Sabine discovered she loved helping street kids. It all started with a young girl named Cookie. Despite being only fourteen, she was the leader of a street gang that dealt hash, LSD, and other drugs.

Cookie came from a Portuguese family with seven children. She'd grown up without a father. She was a hyper, outgoing girl with big brown, saucer eyes. The first time Sabine saw her, she wanted to help her.

She made it a point to visit Cookie and her family on a frequent basis, taking time to talk with her mother and help around the house. Sabine learned that sometimes the gospel was proclaimed best with a bucket of soapy water and a scrub brush. That was the way Sabine related to Cookie and her family.

Certainly, Sabine's life in Brooklyn was poles apart from

being the wife of a millionaire. But by the end of 1975, Sabine again felt the call to move on, this time back to California. Just as The Lord's Land had gone on without her, so now God would continue his work in Brooklyn.

When she returned to Mendocino, she carried a new burden. She wanted to help women in need, women trying to escape abuse and battery. After long hours of thought and prayer, she decided to provide a place of safe haven for them. A place where they could escape from the men who hurt them. A place of healing. And what better place to do this than on The Lord's Land?

So in 1976, Sabine converted the Big House into a refuge of safety. She used part of what she'd gained, selling part of the forest for necessary work on the structure. They remodeled the house, and gave it new furnishings. She wanted it to be a welcoming atmosphere for wounded women.

She named it The Sisters' Home. Even the name would convey a sense of safety and protection. Soon it was ready. Sabine prayed and waited to see whom God would bring to her.

As word of the women's shelter began to spread, well beyond Mendocino, they started to come, bringing their small children with them. Sabine spent the next year living among eight women and many children. All of them were escaping terrible situations.

There was Colette, a Belgian woman whose husband had beaten her for years. She came to The Lord's Land with her three children.

Isabelle was an unwed mother whose boyfriend was now in prison for bank robbery.

Then there was Peggy. Sabine could scarcely believe how

much her boyfriend had abused and traumatized Peggy before she escaped with her two small daughters.

Sabine continually prayed for God's protection. She realized how vulnerable they were to violence at the hands of any one of the abusive husbands or boyfriends.

Always practical, Sabine established a daily routine for everyone to follow. It provided structure and security after the unpredictability and terrors they'd experienced. Every morning at seven, Sabine cheerfully called out, "Sisters, get up!"

After they rolled out of their sleeping bags, they gathered around the wood burning stove to spend the first half hour praying together. Although most weren't used to that, they began to speak freely to God about what they had on their hearts. They also read aloud a few verses from the Bible. Afterward, they tackled their chores, worked in the garden, or did the shopping.

The women adjusted well. An orderly schedule was the first step in regaining their independence and leading a stable life.

Sabine reminded them again and again: "We want to live by God's rules." And together they experienced God blessing their community.

After one year, Colette and Isabelle found work and an apartment together. They had grown beyond needing The Sisters' Home. Now they were able to help others.

One by one, all of the women were able to leave the safe haven of The Sisters' Home. Eventually, everyone had gone.

After she waved goodbye to the last woman and her children, Sabine asked the

Lord, "What do you have for me now?"

She didn't have to wait long. On the same day the last woman left, Sabine received a phone call. It was a pastor in Mendocino. "Is there someone at your place who could look after an old man?"

Sabine smiled. She knew this was God's next assignment. She didn't need to think about it. Something in her spirit knew this was God's will for her. As she had often told the women, "Faith means hearing God's voice and following it."

To her surprise, Sabine learned that Fred–her son who had left her to live with his father in Miami–had become a Christian, too. Now he was in university, training to be a minister.

As for Sabine, welcoming a sick, elderly man to The Lord's Land was only the beginning. She spent the next three years taking in people who were dying. It was difficult work, yet rewarding. What a delight, the way God kept giving her new tasks! His assignments energized her, and taught her even more, drawing on her best talents.

The Lord also kept her wondering what her next challenge would be. In 1980, God surprised Sabine once more. She felt God calling her to return to Germany. She began to remember things from her childhood–things she hadn't thought of in years. She realized it was the Lord, planting the desire to return to the land of her birth.

What was happening in her homeland? Was God working in people's lives there? What about her old friends and acquaintances?

Again after much thought and prayer, Sabine made up her mind. She was going back to Germany. At least for a year or two. The board she had set up would oversee The Lord's Land, as well as the staff she left in charge.

As for Sabine, she could support herself as a housekeeper

while in Germany. She didn't feel shame about her reduced circumstances. Her faith had given her dignity, not only for herself but for any work he called her to do.

A word of scripture came to her mind. "God is with the humble." She didn't have to strive to reach the top any longer. The Lord had shown her: To become great, you have to make yourself small.

It was spring, a good time to start anew. Again, her old schoolfriend Monique met Sabine at the Frankfurt Airport. "It's so good to have you back!" she said, giving her a big hug.

Sabine contacted another old friend, Arvid. He was one of the young people who ate at her table in Santa Barbara. He had returned to Germany, where he gained respect as a computer specialist. Now, he helped Sabine, making an apartment available in his building.

She still needed a job. One day, she and Monique were chatting in a café. Sabine told her the kind of work she was looking for. "I could do the cooking, the cleaning, or mending–whatever a family needs."

Monique sat a little straighter. "I just thought of something. Frau von Stein is looking for someone to help with her sick mother."

"Why does that name sound familiar?" Sabine asked. Then she remembered. "The von Steins were our hosts at the party that night. Remember?"

"Of course!" Monique said. She promised to phone and see if the position was still open.

Later that afternoon, Sabine was sitting in a cozy armchair in Arvid's apartment, reminiscing about their times in Santa Barbara. The telephone rang. He answered, "Ah, hello, Frau von Stein."

Arvid continued speaking, making no attempt to hand her the phone. "Yes, she is here. Certainly, she can come by later," he continued. "What's your address?" He was silent a moment, then looked surprised. "That must be directly behind our building... across the courtyard...."

A minute later, he placed the phone back on the receiver. His eyes were wide. "You're not going to believe this, Sabine. Come over here!" He motioned for her to come into his kitchen.

She followed him to a window. Arvid said, "Remember back in Santa Barbara? You told us a story about going to Herr von Stein's party in his penthouse. You said you saw a washerwoman beside a chestnut tree in a courtyard...."

Sabine looked down and saw a majestic chestnut tree in full bloom, standing below Arvid's window. She was speechless. She was looking down on the same chestnut tree, in the same courtyard she had seen so many years before.

37

I Will Bring You Back and Not Leave You Until I have Done What I Promised You

"I hadn't even noticed that chestnut tree… down there… right behind my apartment…" Arvid stammered, rubbing the back of his neck. "It's *your* chestnut tree!" Sabine stood frozen in place. Across the courtyard, she could see the window where she stood that evening. She had listened to an inner voice saying she could be happy as a washerwoman. She remembered it all now. Herr von Stein's birthday. His collection of paintings. How the simple scene in the courtyard below had been more striking than the most famous art.

And to think, one of her friends, who ate at her table in Santa Barbara, now lived across the same courtyard!

She remembered the words from long ago. *What if I'm to find the meaning of my life as a washerwoman?* How clearly she remembered her answer. *If I find a full life as a washerwoman, then I want to live as a washerwoman.*

Now, here she stood, more than twenty-five years later,

looking down on the chestnut tree, seeking a position as a housekeeper.

When she went to her apartment that evening, Sabine was still stunned. Before going to sleep that night, she prayed. "My God, now I see your handwriting in my life. Thank-you."

She spent the next ten months working as a housekeeper, although not with the von Stein family. She ended up taking another position, in another city—Munich. She joined a church nearby and spent her spare time visiting the sick and elderly. Her days were long and filled with hard work, yet she was wonderfully happy. How ironic that life as a servant filled her with a contentment she hadn't found as one of the most well-to-do ladies in Miami.

In the summer of 1981, Sabine traveled by rail to Berlin. As her train crossed part of East Germany to get to West Berlin, this was Sabine's first time seeing the communist half of her homeland. She was amazed at the contrast between it and West Germany.

Several times, stern officials in uniform passed through the railway car, checking everyone's documents. They had a cold efficiency that reminded Sabine of the Nazi Gestapo.

As she watched towns and countryside roll by, she saw many decrepit houses. There was a drabness, even in summer. The towns reminded Sabine of the terrible years immediately after the war. But Sabine felt something even more dreary. She could sense a spiritual darkness hanging over the land. From what she had heard, the Socialist Unity Party of Germany had clamped down on religious practice, making life difficult for Christians.

On the other hand, as she befriended East German passengers on the train, she felt drawn to them. And once again, something in her spirit stood at attention. She was ready for a new challenge. "Lord, send me here, into the GDR!" she prayed quietly as she watched the countryside go by. It would be years before the Lord took her up on that offer.

*****

After a year in Germany, Sabine returned to California. The decade sped by, as she worked at The Lord's Land, and took various jobs as a housekeeper or a practical nurse.

In 1989, Sabine went to Kona, Hawaii, to receive missionary training at the campus of Youth With A Mission. One morning in November, the YWAM staff set up a TV at the outdoor pavilion. Everyone wanted to see what was happening half a world away, in Berlin, where it was the middle of the night. Sabine watched in amazement as Germans were using sledgehammers, tearing down the Berlin Wall. The television cameras showed East and West Berliners cheering, laughing, and crying. Soon Sabine was crying too.

*****

Scheiss Amis! Scheiss Welt! Scheiss Leben! Someone had sprayed ugly profanity on ruined walls left behind from World War II. Cursing Americans, the world, and life in general, the young people's graffiti radiated anger. Their words saddened Sabine as she walked the streets of Dresden on an overcast summer day in 1992.

The city was located in what used to be communist East Germany. After the Wall came down in 1989, Sabine had eagerly followed reports of the reunification of East and West Germany. But it was three years before she could come for a visit, and see for herself.

Now she could scarcely believe she was here. And in Dresden. Memories came rushing back. She and Hans running through the streets during *carnivale...* cowering in the Schlüter's cellar during the fire bombing… escaping the walls of flame and the smell of burning flesh.

So much had changed in forty-seven years. And yet, some places looked like the war had just ended. As Sabine walked, surveying the shabby neighborhood, she saw the graffiti for what it was: the pain of adolescent souls, spilling onto walls and buildings.

A wave of sadness swept over her. She passed what had to be the local hangout of young people. Several teenagers slouched against the building. They all had eyes that showed despair. Somehow Sabine knew that they expected nothing more from life.

Sabine continued down the street. Posters plastered on walls and windows announced upcoming events—punk concerts, or movies with pornography, violence, and occult themes. Where was the hope? Tears sprang to her eyes. "Lord," she prayed, "these young people must break your heart, too."

For a long while, she prayed as she walked. As she did, she felt a determination to bring hope to this city. But she was sixty-eight years old. Was she too old to start something new?

When she flew back to California, she couldn't shake the feeling God was once again calling her. The first thing she did when she arrived back in Mendocino was set up a meeting with her pastor and the leaders of her church. Sabine feared she was too old for a new undertaking. But when she told them about Dresden, her friends and church members reassured her. She could do everything because Christ was giving her strength.

She would have to rely on God. For one thing, she had poured everything she owned into the ministry of The Lord's

Land.

However, when Sabine told God she would trust him, again, she realized she had already made her decision. She was moving to Dresden.

In addition to her regular work on The Lord's Land, she began to take various jobs in San Francisco. She stayed with friends and saved money for the return to Germany.

By now, The Lord's Land had become a popular Christian retreat center. Although she'd hate to leave her cottage among the redwoods, she knew the property was in capable hands. Responsible staff ran the ministry, and Sabine trusted its board of directors wholeheartedly.

As for her sons, they were living their own lives. Fred was now a pastor. Cliff was an insurance salesman. Both were married, and each had two children.

There was nothing holding Sabine back. Even though many her age had long since retired, she was ready to embark on a new adventure. She told everyone at her farewell party, "The German youth desperately need hope."

Her initial plan was to stay in Germany a year. There was no way she could have known that a decade later, she would be struggling with the greatest challenge of her life.

38

Preach the Gospel to All Creation

In January of 1993, Sabine arrived in Dresden, carrying two small suitcases, and the equivalent of fifteen hundred dollars (three thousand deutschmark). The gloom of her new neighborhood shocked her. Regularly, she walked along Louisenstrasse, the main street, trying in her spirit to overcome the heavy despair that shrouded everything. Torn curtains hung in windows with broken panes. It looked like a tide of trash had washed up on curbs and filled empty lots. Graffiti with gang symbols, profanity, and hateful words seemed to mar every house and building.

How could these young people have any hope? she wondered again as she walked down the depressing streets.

She couldn't wait to get to work, telling youth about the hope Jesus gives. Sabine moved into an apartment on Frülingstrasse. The lead member of a rock band, Höllenhunde (The Hell Hounds), lived right across the hall. She knew she'd come to the right place.

Martin-Luther-Strasse, the center of Dresden Neustadt, was only a fifteen-minute walk from her apartment. One day, as she was passing along that street, she saw an old building standing next to a Lutheran church.

She already knew she wanted to start a café and a second-hand store. Now as she stood in front of Number 12 Martin-Luther-Strasse, she realized this was the perfect location. When she asked around, Sabine found the city owned it. The building had formerly housed a schnapps store. But now no one seemed interested in renting retail space in this area. Even the schnapps store had long since failed.

Sabine was able to rent two rooms on the ground floor, with an entrance on the street corner. The rent was a thousand deutschmark per month. Since she only had about three thousand deutschmark, she'd have to trust God for the rent.

She was going to need a lot of help. So Sabine went to many churches in Dresden, describing her goal. In addition to financial support, Sabine asked for energetic, believing youth to tackle the project with her. Many were eager to help. They came from a variety of churches, including two young Catholic volunteers.

They started immediately. Almost every day, hard working young people were sawing, hammering, patching, and painting. The rooms transformed quickly. Every week it was something new: A carpenter installed a suspended ceiling. An engineer updated the electricity. Several churches gave money and donated furnishings, including a refrigerator, chairs, and scratched, yet sturdy wooden tables. They lovingly repaired and cleaned each item. Sabine wanted everything to be charming and comfortable, welcoming everyone who came.

In April of 1993, the café opened its doors. She named it Stoffwechsel, from two German words: *stoff* meaning "fabric" or "material," and *wechel* meaning "exchange." People were to come just as they were, encounter Jesus, and leave with a changed life.

"We should receive anyone who walks through these doors with love," she told her coworkers. "We should treat everyone with love, the way Jesus loved and accepted us."

Soon, the smell of fresh cake wafted from 12 Martin-Luther-Strasse. They served free coffee and tea, as well as cookies and rolls. Next door to the café, visitors could browse in the secondhand clothing shop.

It didn't take long for word to spread. The disadvantaged, the homeless, drug addicts, punks, goths, and young people of all sorts filled the place. As Sabine watched how fast it took shape, she realized how many years she had wasted. She would have become a Christian sooner if she had seen churches working together like this, helping those who needed it. Their Bibles weren't sitting on a shelf somewhere gathering dust. They were living its message in Dresden. Sabine thought, *If only every city had a place like this!* Believers could stop judging their city's young people and start reaching out to them.

For the rest of her life, Sabine wanted to encourage Christians to use the strength God had already given them to do whatever he showed them to do.

In Dresden, the volunteers set out a generous buffet every Saturday. They invited everyone in the community to come eat, for free. This would have cost too much without the help of the Dresdner Tafel–a charitable organization that collected food from stores. Also, the baker across the street donated fresh rolls.

God was reinventing Sabine from being a mother to California hippies, to being a mother for Dresden's street kids.

She knew changes in Dresden Neustadt would take longer. But from now on, there was someone here for the young people—someone who would give them unconditional love and support.

Sabine wanted to understand the young people she was trying to help. So, just as she had done years before in Haight-Ashbury, she went to study youth in their environment. She decided to attend some rock concerts.

She'd be the only seventy-year-old there, but that didn't stop her. One event was held inside a former leather factory that was about to be demolished. Sabine walked in to the roars and growls of electric guitars, the thunder of drums, and the screams of singers. In Sabine's mind, the bands were producing a hellish racket. Despite her earplugs, she worried that she'd lose her hearing. Flashing strobe lights disoriented her vision, and she dodged some young men who started throwing themselves against one another. She thought at first they were fighting. She learned it was called "slam dancing."

As strobes burst on and off, she tried to find familiar faces from the café. Eventually, she recognized some, leaning against a rusty pipe at the edge of the crowd. Most were dressed all in black. Some had tattoos, and piercings in their nose, lips, and brow.

However, even here, where people were supposed to be having a good time, the look on their faces brought Sabine to tears. She wasn't being sentimental. It was God, giving her the ability to see into their souls, to see how broken and alone they were. She felt like her heart was literally coming apart.

39

God is Love/Gott ist Leibe

S abine wiped her tears and went over to a group of girls and hugged them, not saying a thing.

Then she spoke to a young boy wearing an upside-down crucifix around his neck. "Don't throw your life away!" she said. "You're precious. There's hope for your life."

She had learned not to ask, "How are you?" When she asked that, either they ignored her, or snarled, "Mind your own business, Grandma!"

She wanted to share kindness with these young people–to show them the love of Christ. And she invited each one to the café.

Every morning, before the café opened, Sabine prayed with her coworkers. They were careful to name each individual who had come to the café, asking God to reveal his love to them. They also prayed for every encounter God would give them that day. And Sabine was blessed with many encounters.

There was Marion. Her uncle raped her when she was twelve. Now she was fourteen, living with a boyfriend twice her age. She often came to the café and poured her heart out to Sabine. But Marion was never able to escape her lifestyle.

Another was Mo, a gorgeous young woman with two small children and many lovers. She didn't know where the fathers of her children were. One day, she rushed into the café trembling violently. One of her boyfriends had hidden drugs in her refrigerator and disappeared.

A friend telephoned Mo, warning that several men were waiting in her apartment—probably the Mafia. Sabine hid the young woman and her children in a safe place, out of the city.

Years later, Mo said during a television interview, "No one believed me. No one. Sabine was the first person who believed what I said. She believed in me."

Sabine helped Mo believe in God, too. Mo began to pray. It was a long process, but slowly she learned to trust God. Later, she even married. Order came into Mo's life, and so much healing with it.

*****

More than sixteen years have passed since Sabine moved to Dresden and took on her toughest challenge yet. In some ways, trying to reach German young people is similar to what she faced in California among hippies in the seventies. But in other ways, what urban youth face today is far worse.

The diminutive, white-haired lady has changed, too. Her wealthy friends in Miami wouldn't recognize Sabine now. Her faith has been forged in trials and difficulties. She has faced physical threats and hate. At times, violence has broken out in the coffee house at 12 Martin-Luther-Strasse. They've had to replace four big windows when neighbors hurled stones through them.

Sabine is often the only one standing between the young people and destruction. Once, a boy was nearly beaten to death in Stoffwechsel. She was alone in the café when a pack of thugs followed the boy in and began to beat him up. As he fell to the floor, they jumped on him and continued to punch and kick.

There was little an older woman could do to stop them. The hoodlums didn't stop beating him until the ambulance and paramedics arrived. After the boy was in the hospital, Sabine visited him throughout his slow recovery.

Because of incidents such as this, the neighbors do not always speak fondly of Stoffwechsel. But she shows kindness to them, just as she does to the street kids who come to the café. Her "children," as she refers to them, aren't always easy to love. One minute, they embrace and kiss her. The next, they might throw eggs at the café, or scratch the Stoffwechsel bus.

If a regular guest suddenly stops coming, Sabine usually finds them in prison. Either they've broken into a car, held up a store, or got caught trafficking drugs. Many times, she is the only person who visits them.

She tells them about the life she has lived, of how she always tried to achieve more, and how she had once lived the life of a multimillionaire. She tells of the emptiness she felt, despite everything. And she tells about her guilt. Then, she shares how she came to Jesus, the Man on the Cross. His death paid the penalty for her guilt, and his resurrection gave her new life.

There's no such thing as a hopeless case for God, she tells them. Whatever they've done, in God's eyes they're infinitely precious.

The work of Stoffwechsel has continued to grow. Donations from the community and throughout Germany have allowed the ministry to expand. A big leap forward came when Sabine learned about 29 Martin-Luther-Strasse.

Neighbors told Sabine about this deserted building down the street. It was slated for demolition. Area residents didn't relish the idea of another large, impersonal block of apartments going up in its place.

Even though the structure was falling into ruin, Sabine saw possibilities. They had done such a good job fixing up their store and café. Their staff and volunteers would also put love into this renovation, making it a place of hope for the neighborhood. And the additional space would allow them to help many more young people, and children.

She took her ideas to the staff of Stoffwechsel, and they spent much time in prayer. Was this what God wanted them to do next?

Since the city owned 29 Martin-Luther-Strasse, Sabine decided to write the mayor. Using her best stationery, she addressed her letter to Dr. Herbert Wagner, Mayor of Dresden.

She wrote about being a practicing Christian, and how she'd spent years working with young people in California. Sabine shared how she started the work at Stoffwechsel, and how they were helping Dresden's youth, encouraging them to turn away from drugs.

She finished by telling about the vacant building, how they would like to fix it up, and rent two suites to expand their ministry.

The mayor invited her to meet with him. To Sabine's joy, he agreed to a change of plans for the old property. When she brought back a lease agreement, her staff at Stoffwechsel jumped up and down, shouting, "Praise God!" and "Hallelujah!"

"What's more," Sabine said, pacing around in excitement, "I was able to tell him what we're doing in the city!" She sat down at a table, smiling and shaking her head. "That was God," Sabine said, summing up the victory at city hall. "It's God who cares for us like that."

A large staff, as well as interns, and even a civil servant now belong to the Stoffwechsel team. Ralf Knauthe—known affectionately as Knaffi—is the leader of the work. Thurid, who goes by the nickname "Master Chef," and many other faithful workers are moving into new areas and new ways of reaching young people. Their motto: "We venture out in faith."

A number of political and social leaders have also lent their support, including the former Prime Minister's wife, Ingrid Biedenkopf, and the Minister for Social Affairs, Christine Weber. Sabine has been honored many times for her work. She uses each opportunity to tell of "her children," and how much God cares for them.

Sabine's sons, Cliff and Fred are both married now, with two children each. She tries to see them once a year.

The work that began when Sabine arrived with two suitcases and fifteen hundred dollars has attracted reporters from TV, radio, newspapers, and magazines. They've done interviews and documentaries on "the little miracle in the middle of Dresden."

Once a television station sent her a first class ticket, flying her in for an interview. She traded it for a coach seat. She said, "It was impossible for the mother of street kids to fly first class!"

Sabine only owns a couple of outfits. She usually pairs them with a light blue blouse and a rose brooch made of silk. Her life among the street kids still piques the curiosity of visitors. They ask…

"How did you come to live here?"

"Is it true you were a millionaire?"

"How did you do all this?"

Most furrow their brows when Sabine answers, "It's God who does it. Without him, I couldn't do anything at all. But, one thing I'm certain of… His work here in Dresden is far from finished."

"I have seen all the things that are done under the sun; all of them are meaningless, a chasing after the wind."

Ecclesiastes 1:14

40

Postscript by Frederick (Fred) Ball

On the evening of July 6, 2009, I had what would be my final talk with my mother. She told me about her latest speaking engagement in Munich and how she tried to teach others about loving young people who were in the punk rock culture. She had taken a long trip on the train back to her flat in Dresden. She said that she was quite tired but always enjoyed talking with me. In fact, we had grown quite close through the years because of our common relationship with the presence of Jesus.

I told her about the new church to which I had been appointed. She cautioned me about becoming too enthusiastic and reminded me of my life experiences in the other seven churches I had pastored. However, I could tell that she was quite proud of the way my family and I were carrying on Christ's ministry that was begun through her life.

At the end of our conversation, she spoke one of the most perfect prayers I ever heard from another individual and then we concluded our talk by telling each other how much we loved one another. I could have not asked for a better final conversation between two individuals. Five hours later, my mother Sabine Ball was translated from this earthly life to be forever with the One whom she adored more than all: Jesus Christ.

As I understand it, my telephone call from Lake Placid, Florida to her apartment in Dresden, Germany was the last conversation my mother had with anyone on this earth. For the last half of an hour of my mother's life, she was heard to have repeated the words: "Jesus, Jesus, Jesus…" The following week, her funeral service was held in Cross Church, (*Kruez Kirche*) with the company of over 1,300 Dresdeners, East Germans, Germans, and people from all over this world. Although people had referred to her as "The Mother Theresa of Dresden" she told me in our final conversation: **"I just want to be known as 'Sabine, a Christian.'"**

To the friends of Sabine who attended and made her work possible, my family and I are deeply grateful for continuing her work (and especially to her friends in Youth with a Mission as well as *Stoffwechsel* in Dresden, Germany). It is the intent that all profits will be given to my mother's charity foundation in Germany: *Stoffwechsel* (pronounced shtough' Veckzel – which means exchange).

Photographs

Sabine, on right, with her sister Marianne

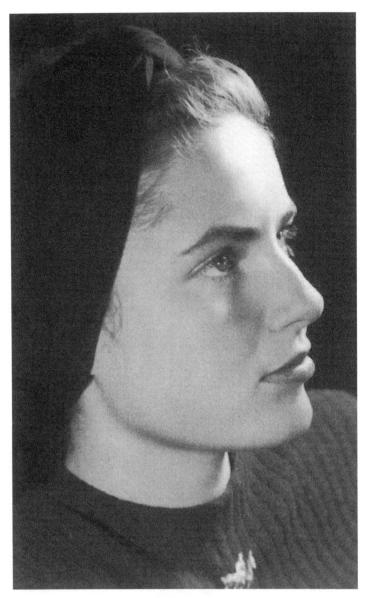

Sabine 1945

Sabine and Cliff are married, March 1953

Monks and students at the monastery in 1971. Thubten Yeshe is third from the right.

The Woodbutcher Cabin at the Lord's Land with Sabine

Sabine's Baptism

Early days at The Lord's Land with Sabine at the far left

Sabine, in back second from right, with friends in Brooklyn
1974-75

Sabine at the Lord's Land with her grandson, Joshua

Sabine entering Stoffwechsel

Sabine with Ralf Knauthe in 2008. Ralf is current chairman of Stoffwechsel.

Sabine with her son, Fred, and his family, Summer 2007

*Sabine in the Big House with the light breaking through
(inspiration for book title & cover image)*

Memories of Sabine

From Tomás Dertner ~ Lay minister and friend to Sabine since 1970

I was destined to meet Sabine Ball as evidenced by not one, but two hitchhiking opportunities within the span of a single day back in 1970. I passed up the first offer of a ride because I was too lazy (and stoned) to get up from my sunny spot, so she sped off in a huff only to inadvertently stop for me several hours later. Once she discovered it was the lazy bum, she wanted to take off, but I was already moving the contents of her car aside to make room and I jumped in. I launched into speaking German with her (my second language) and that eased the strain of our first few moments. Thus started the biggest and best adventure of my life.

She was interested in anyone and everyone and always picked up strays beside the road. For her, it was not unlike gold mining of a different kind, finding people who were like minded and wanted to work to make the world a better place. When we met, she owned a large property on the Mendocino Coast and was open to sharing it with industrious souls who wanted to get back to the land, explore the arts and share all things in common. I was with her before and after the spiritual awakening that came in 1972, but her heart only became bigger and broader after the transition. In 1974, we both signed up to help start a street ministry in New York City, with a small group of believers, and later she returned to her native Germany to reach out to lost souls on the streets of Dresden. I traveled to Dresden in 2004 and saw her in action there and was made aware of the trust and favor bestowed upon her and her staff by the city officials for the charitable work she was doing. She was always single-minded in her life's work, to connect with people one on one to determine if she could encourage them to dig deep within themselves, to discover the God who had created them, and then to serve Him by using their particular gifts. She fed countless people, both literally and spiritually and until her dying day never passed up an opportunity to speak to a person on the street, no matter how scraggly they looked or how late the hour. She had the heart of God for each and every person and I consider myself supremely blessed to have met her, to have been mentored by her and to continue her legacy of reaching out, one worthy and beautiful soul at a time.

From Kathleen Krohn ~ followed Sabine to Germany to help begin ministry

I came to know Sabine one night sitting at the campfire on her property in Mendocino, The Lord's Land. I had known of her because of our common experience of speaking German and knowing the culture, after visiting the retreat for several years. As we sat singing and story-telling around the campfire, she reached over and asked me if I would like to go with her to Germany and start a mission, and if I could stay over the next day I would be able to hear her announce her plans. So of course I had to stay and hear what this adventure was all about!

Four months later I am following her to Dresden, Germany to help her start what was to be called Cafe Stoffwechsel. When I arrived she had already made contact with five churches, secured an apartment, and had just prayed with a woman, who became her soundingboard for all major appointments and correspondence with the city, over a corner store that had been vacant. Sabine knew how to get things done, she was tenacious, humble, and strategic in her goal setting. She was winsome in recruiting help, humble with strangers, mysterious when telling her testimony, and accommodating with the pre-christians. She had a distinct style and became famous very quickly!

She never missed a beat, whether it was Holy Spirit directing her or her own intuition (also God's gifting), she networked strategically and consistently. Living with her, I usually didn't even know half of what was coming next! Many times she would say, I just don't know how such and such should be done, but then soon enough she was bringing in the supplies to accomplish that very thing. In one year, she had a team of 12 volunteers, who were all assigned different days to work with her in the store, one of whom would become her right-hand man, director and successor, Ralf Knauthe, for the whole project to this day. She contacted the city many times to pitch her project and vision to help the poor, the children and the community several times, thus landing two abandoned apartment complexes joined by an inner courtyard, smack dab in the middle of the community she was reaching. She was interviewed for newspapers, magazines, was invited on talk shows and became known as "the Mother Teresa of Dresden". I was dazzled by the favor, grace and common cause she walked in. The ministry goes on today as a social reform reaching children and families, after celebrating its 25th anniversary in 2018.

Unfortunately, Sabine wanted more of me than I could be, namely to be like her, minister like her, and carry the vision like her. After my one year commitment we parted on uneasy terms. I moved to the Lord's Land to fill a vacant position in housekeeping and we would see each other every year when she came to visit her home. These visits remained just that, a yearly visit as she made Dresden her permanent home. My husband at the time, an interior refinisher of the finest taste, remodeled her chosen cabin on the Lord's Land. Therefore, after reconciling our differences we continued to make her visit a priority every summer. The anticipation of hearing her exciting stories and all the Lord was doing through her to form a lasting presence in the suburbs of Dresden never ended........there was always more, expansion, new ways to evangelize and never a shortage of people who wanted to help and get involved.

Sabine showed me so much of God's heart for His daughter and for anyone that will step out to go on a great adventure with Him. I am encouraged to this day to risk, ask for more, and trust the Lord to carry me in the unknown of advancing His Kingdom. At her memorial, in one of the old cathedrals of Dresden, the Sisters Church, it seemed so perfect for her to be remembered. Where she once escaped from, there she returned giving back the love, freedom and spirit she had discovered in her great adventure called life!

From Ralf Knauthe ~ Co-founder and Chairman of Stoffwechsel

Sabine often raved about people she'd meet. I remember once how she once enthusiastically told about a young man she had met on the street here in our district and the qualities that she saw in him - he was a leader, a real leader, someone whose voice rises for truth and shapes people. A few weeks later I came to Sabine's room and she had a visitor. Sabine introduced him to me, mentioning that it was this man she had told me about. At first I was "shocked" inside. Up until then I had a completely different picture. It didn't match the person in front of me at all. I saw a man strongly influenced by alcohol and prison, whose highlight of his life was the streets. He was the leader of a group that regulary sat around a youth club in the district, drank too much alcohol and often argued loudly. A person you otherwise tend to avoid in everyday life.

However, Sabine's gaze said 'here is a valuable person loved by God.' She first saw the beauty of God in him and not the "dirt" on him. She could do this because she knew from her own experience what is possible through God's love. Up until the age of 46, Sabine had been searching for the meaning of life - until God's love found her heart in a profound way. And this love changed her life from a seeker for her own happiness to a finder who was now looking for people with whom to share this happiness: I have been found by God's love, He is my Heavenly Father and I am His beloved daughter. Sabine often said, "I love people, but not sin in their lives. I don't agree with them in everything, but I understand them. And I don't want to judge them, but to see them with God's eyes and accept them with His love."

237

That was Sabine's heart. She was moved by God's love for and towards people, she was enthusiastic about them, loved them, listened and spoke encouraging words into their lives.

For almost 17 years I had the privilege of working with Sabine in my hometown of Dresden to serve people. Sabine's courageous move to Dresden also moved my life. With her love and devotion to God and to people, she also deeply shaped my heart. When Sabine signed her books, she always wrote these words: *Gott ist Liebe* (God is love). I once asked her why she was doing this. Sabine replied, "I haven't come up with anything better and it sums it up wonderfully." So for me these three words express what Sabine lived and was known for: God is love. It is so encouraging that today we can draw from the same source Sabine lived from - the love of God and the power of his Spirit. In this manner Sabine's legacy lives on today - God's love working through people like you and me, here on earth. *Gott ist Liebe.*

From Erin Dertner ~ long-time friend

Sabine had been one of our dearest friends for over 40 years by the time she left the earth. I met her at age 18 when my mom and siblings made a trip to the Mendocino Coast and she remained as close as could be. She attended our wedding in 1978, was at the birth of our 2nd son, and was involved in both our sons' lives as they grew up. She made a huge imprint on each one of us.

She was a person that looked you in the eye and bored a hole into your soul. There was no hiding from her and this was one of her greatest strengths. She knew how to seize the moment with anyone and everyone, not knowing if she would have the opportunity again to express the urgency of what was on her heart at any given time. She called each person up to their personal best, to walk in a manner that was pleasing to the Lord and to put away vain pursuits that got in the way of that goal. She was truly one of a kind and made sure each person's life that she encountered was challenged and blessed.

From Rense Miller ~ long-time friend

In 1969 I went AWOL from the Air Force and hitchhiked from Biloxi, MS to Fort Bragg, CA. I was wandering around town and ran into my friend Pete so we decided to hitchhike to Mendocino. Because it was my birthday, Pete decided to give me some illegal substance for a present. The next thing we know a Highway Patrolman pulled up to question us. We both were really scared. Just then this lady, Sabine, in a yellow Toyota station wagon pulled up and said, "Officer, these boys are my friends and I was going to give them a ride home." Needless to say my first experience with this wonderful woman was very special and life changing.

From Caren Linden ~ long-time friend

I'm not sure what year this memory happened but it must have been either 1982 or '83. It was early in the day; Sabine and I were talking by the clothesline when Art Katz walked up. My impression at the time was that he was coming to say goodbye after spending a day or two resting at the Lord's Land. At the time, it was not an official retreat center and guests were welcomed for a donation. He walked toward us very purposefully and said, *"Sabine! When the Berlin Wall comes down, you will go back to Germany and you will be used to testify about Jesus's love to government officials, even to the highest!"* That was it! It was not said with a "the Lord told me to bring this word to you" or any fanfare like that. However, it came with a great deal of certainty; enough that it made an indelible impression on my mind; enough so that I remembered when the Berlin Wall did indeed come down November 9, 1989. And as we all know, Sabine did indeed go back to her native land and was used mightily there, even to the highest government officials.

Chapter Title References

The manuscript Sabine left did not have titles for the chapters. She had plans to work with her son, Fred, to complete these and other details in the book the summer of 2009. Fred, a "retiring" minister, kindly offered these verses when asked to help with the titles. The reader is encouraged to read the verses in their larger context.

1. You are My Hiding Place from **Psalm 32:7**
2. Every Thing is Meaningless from **Ecclesiastes 1:2**
3. We Wait in Hope for the Lord from **Psalm 33:20**
4. I Reduced You to Ashes from **Ezekiel 28:18**
5. The Lord is Good from **Lamentations 3:25**
6. You are My Refuge from **Psalm 142:5**
7. Where Your Treasure Is from **Matthew 6:21**
8. A Friend Loves at all Times from **Proverbs 17:17**
9. There is Nothing Better Than to Enjoy One's Work from **Ecclesiastes 3:22**
10. He Has Brought Down Rulers from Their Thrones from **Luke 1:51-52**
11. Charm is Deceptive and Beauty is Fleeting from **Proverbs 31:30**
12. Wide is the Gate and Broad is the Road that Leads to Destruction from **Matthew 7:13**

13. Unless the Lord Builds the House, the Builders Labor in Vain from **Psalm 127:1**
14. See How the Flowers of the Field Grow from **Matthew 6:28-29**
15. My Life is But a Breath from **Job 7:7**
16. Wine is a Mocker and Beer a Brawler from **Proverbs 20:1**
17. I Am With You and Will Watch Over You from **Genesis 28:15**
18. They are Disheartened, Troubled Like the Restless Sea from **Jeremiah 49:23**
19. Seek and You Will Find from **Matthew 7:7**
20. Watch Out for False Prophets from **Matthew 7:15**
21. Guard Your Heart from **Proverbs 4:23**
22. Your Wisdom and Knowledge Mislead You from **Isaiah 47:10**
23. The Wise Woman Builds Her House from **Proverbs 14:1**
24. Children Sitting in the Marketplaces from **Matthew 11:16**
25. I Have Raised You Up for This Very Purpose from **Exodus 9:16**
26. Do Not Worry About Your Life from **Matthew 6:25**
27. I Will Bring You Back to This Land from **Genesis 28:15**
28. I Have Promised to Bring You Out of Your Misery from **Exodus 3:17**
29. No One Does Good, Not Even One from **Romans 3:12**
30. Out of the Depths I Cry to You from **Psalm 130:1**
31. The Fool Says in his Heart, "There is no God." from **Psalm 14:1**
32. I Am The Way and The Truth and The Life from **John 14:6**

33. Jesus is Lord from **Romans 10:9**

34. Confess Your Sins and Pray for Each Other from **James 5:16**

35. How Can They Hear without Someone Preaching to Them? from **Romans 10:14**

36. You Will be My Witnesses…to the Ends of the Earth from **Acts 1:8**

37. I Will Not Leave You Until I Have Done What I Have Promised from **Genesis 28:15**

38. Preach Gospel to All Creation from **Mark 16:15**

39. God is Love/Gott ist Leibe from **1 John 4:8**

Acknowledgments

This has been a *labor of love,* as Sabine used to say, meaning it has been completed because those involved have a love for Jesus, and also for Sabine. All profits and proceeds from this publication go to the ongoing work of Stoffwechsel (stoffwechsel.org), the ministry Sabine began in Germany. Apart from the manuscript which Sabine worked on with a professional author, most of the other material has been gathered from friends, family and online research. It is truly impossible to give credit to original sources since so much has been shared among Sabine's friends and family. In the end, I think Sabine would like it this way, giving all the credit, glory, honor and praise to Jesus Christ, the author and finisher of our faith.

Stoffwechsel and Further Information

To learn more about Stoffwechsel

Website:
  https://stoffwechsel.org

Address:
  Stoffwechsel e.V.
  Martin-Luther-Str. 29
  01099 Dresden
  Germany

Phone:
  +49 351 21527300

Email:
  info@stoffwechsel.org

The Sabine Ball Foundation Website:
  https://sabine-ball-stiftung.de/h.html

For further information about the Lord's Land:

YWAM Mendocino Coast at the Lord's Land has a website: http://ywammendocino.org

Please "visit" and "like" the Facebook page for *Love Broke Through by Sabine Ball*. It is a space for book updates and more importantly a place to share your memories of Sabine and connect with others who have stories to tell. Go to: **https://www.facebook.com/lovebrokethroughbysabineball/**

Made in the USA
Coppell, TX
04 October 2020